by the
Mead Public Library

6/93

A

Adult Services
Mead Public Library
Sheboygan, Wisconsin

Borrowers are responsible for all library
materials drawn on their cards and for all
charges accruing on same.

DEMCO

Also by Loretta Schwartz-Nobel

A Mother's Story (with Mary Beth Whitehead)

Engaged to Murder

Starving in the Shadow of Plenty

The Baby Swap Conspiracy

FORSAKING
ALL OTHERS

FORSAKING ALL OTHERS

•••

THE REAL
BETTY BRODERICK
STORY

Including Prison Interviews

•••

Loretta Schwartz-Nobel

VILLARD BOOKS
New York
1993

For Joel, with whom I share
the time to create,
the freedom to grow,
and the joy of a son.

All rights reserved under International and Pan-American
Copyright Conventions. Published in the United States by Villard
Books, a division of Random House, Inc., New York, and
simultaneously in Canada by Random House of Canada Limited,
Toronto.

Villard Books is a registered trademark of Random House, Inc.

Library of Congress Cataloging-in-Publication Data
Schwartz-Nobel, Loretta.
Forsaking all others: the real Betty Broderick story; including
prison interviews/Loretta Schwartz-Nobel.
p.   cm.
ISBN 0-679-41601-3
1. Broderick, Betty. 2. Murderers—California—Biography.
3. Murder—California—Case studies. I. Title.
HV6248.B7277S38 1993   364.1'523'092—dc20   92-38366
[B]

Manufactured in the United States of America on acid-free paper

9 8 7 6 5 4 3 2

First Edition

AUTHOR'S NOTE

Much of the dialogue in this book has been taken directly from court transcripts. In certain cases it has been reconstructed from interviews with the people who were directly involved.

Some scenes have been dramatically re-created in order to portray the emotions and feelings more effectively. The names of a few minor characters have been changed to protect their privacy.

In all cases I have tried to be as accurate as possible. When there were conflicting versions of events, I have chosen to present Betty Broderick's point of view, since this book is an attempt to bring the reader into her world.

ACKNOWLEDGMENTS

This book could not have been written without the inspiration of my agent, Ellen Levine; the judgment of my editor, Diane Reverand; and the assistance of my typist, Janice Hughes.

I want to thank Irene Schaffer for her insight into the La Jolla scene and Dave Hall for making San Diego a second home.

I'd like to express my love and gratitude to my husband, Dr. Joel Nobel; his children, Josh and Erika; my sons' babysitter, Rosemary Gross; my mother, Fay Rosenberg; and my children, Ruth, Rebecca, and Adam.

I will always be grateful to Betty Broderick for helping me understand.

CONTENTS

Author's Note   vii

Acknowledgments   ix

Introduction   xiii

PART I   Till Death Do Us Part   1

PART II   The Early Years   19

PART III   The Affair   55

PART IV   Fury   101

PART V   Over the Edge   133

PART VI   The Trials   169

PART VII   Life Today   225

Epilogue   233

INTRODUCTION

There was something about the Central California Women's Facility that made me feel I was stepping over the jagged edge of the earth I knew into another world.

It started with the long drive from the tiny Fresno airport in the hot, dry desert heat. Maybe it was the barrenness of the endless road that leads to the prison, with nothing, absolutely nothing but flat, hot brown dust on either side.

That surreal mood set the stage for the tall razor-wire fences that rose out of the ground, equipped with electronic motion sensors, and the huge control tower that seemed to grow there out of the dead earth when nothing else would. It operated the opening and the closing of the giant iron gates.

Maybe it was knowing that every move I made was being transmitted to security vehicles for immediate response in case that was necessary.

Maybe it was just realizing that beyond those fences and towers and armed guards, there were 1,628 women who couldn't leave, locked up, controlled, and guarded, primarily by men.

I was frightened as I parked the rented red Pinto, but I knew that there was no place, absolutely no place I would rather be than entering that prison for the first of a three-day visit with Betty Broderick.

I surrendered my purse, my necklace, my watch, my keys, and my wedding ring. I removed my shoes and had my body searched.

Finally, carrying a clear plastic bag of one-dollar bills for the vending machines, a pen, a notebook, and a tape recorder, I stepped through a set of doors into a fenced, electronically controlled tunnel. It felt like a cage. I looked up at the tower as I waited for the doors to open, knowing they would soon shut behind me. Then, for the moment, I, too, would be locked in.

When Betty was finally led through a door by an armed guard on the other side of a huge room, she hugged me and smiled. I was her first visitor. "My God," I said, once we were seated in a small conference room, "I can't believe we're really here."

"You're only visiting, honey," she said.

I had seen her every day for eight weeks during her second trial, but except for brief phone calls we had never really had a chance to talk.

She was warm, friendly, and surprisingly relaxed. She said that in prison she had begun to heal. From time to time we took a break, shut off the tape recorder, and walked out of the little conference room usually reserved for attorneys, into the visitors' section, where other prisoners sat with their husbands, mothers, children, or friends.

Sometimes as we wandered toward the vending machines, Betty would stop and chat, or introduce me to the women who had become her friends. Except for the guards and the locked doors, the visiting area with its round metal tables looked almost like an institutional cafeteria. The place was, as Betty put it, "brand-spanking-new and very sterile."

"As long as I keep the frame of mind that this is fascinating, I'm okay," she explained. "I keep saying to myself, 'Isn't this interesting? Isn't this incredible?' The worst part is the long distance from my children. I'm trying to change that. There is a law in my favor that says a first-time offender will be placed closest to home. So far, with me, they just won't do it."

Most mothers and divorced women identify with some part of Betty Broderick's story. It's a gut-level identification that cuts to the very core of how we were raised. Men were valued for what they did, women for how they looked. For me it began with a newspaper article and two photographs in *The New York Times*.

In the first, Dan Broderick was standing, wineglass in hand, toasting a gorgeous young Marla Maples–type blonde. Her head was thrown back, her hair flowed over her shoulders. They were both laughing. Next to them was a small photo insert of Betty Broderick, a heavy, middle-aged woman, all alone. She was crying.

For women all over America those photographs stirred memories and evoked old fears.

Men's reactions were different. Money, power, and beautiful young women are still the standard male rewards.

My own husband's response was typical. He smiled approvingly. "Beautiful woman," he said, pointing to Dan's new wife. "The first one was crazy."

"Do you really think so?" I asked.

"Absolutely," he answered. "By her logic you would have killed your first husband and his new wife."

"I guess that's true," I said. In some ways our stories were remarkably similar.

I, like Betty, was part of a generation of girls raised to believe that someday our prince would come. He would marry us, complete us, and we'd live happily ever after.

We needed no self-esteem, no core of individual identity, no personal strength. All we needed was a strong, successful man. In marriage our boundaries would merge. They would flow into each other. His strength and success would be ours. We would be one forever.

Poets, philosophers, and psychiatrists have long said that in the best lovemaking we could lose ourselves briefly, but when Betty was growing up, girls were being told that this ideal state, this interpenetrating mix-up, this lack of boundaries, could last a lifetime. All we needed to do was find the right boy and become his wife.

Like Betty, I found a prince who was planning to become a doctor. I saw him through college and medical school, military service, and internship. Fourteen years and two children later I watched him walk out and "marry" a beautiful blonde while he was still married to me. He didn't pay child support.

I never got over it, but I didn't kill him. Most women don't. The scars are there, but we heal enough to move on.

Clearly Betty Broderick's story touched a raw nerve in me. I wondered what made her different.

Dan's brother, Larry, claimed that Betty was a monster, obsessed by hatred. Some of her neighbors called her materialistic and said it was money and status she grieved for, not her lost husband or children.

For each person who condemned Betty, another stepped forward to say that she was the most devoted, beautiful, cheerful, committed, adoring young wife and mother they had ever known.

Perhaps in the complexity of Betty's behavior many of us saw some part of ourselves. The conflicts and contradictions that tormented Betty Broderick defined the human struggle.

When the first trial ended in a hung jury with Walter Polk, a sixty-two-year-old male juror, saying, "Yes, she shot him. I just wondered what took her so long," the press went wild.

"No case has generated this much public interest in ten years," said Dan Shafer, news director at KNSD-TV, where portions of the trial were broadcast live as a result of huge public demand.

"It's become a morality play for the community," explained sociologist Gordon Clanton. "People just can't stop talking about it. It's a social phenomenon."

Helen Fleming, a California woman drinking coffee at a La Jolla café, said, "Betty did something important for scores of women, because the next Dan Broderick will think twice before he acts. Sometimes you need a little prairie justice."

Whether people saw her as a new folk heroine, a victim, or a crazy, vindictive lady, Betty Broderick triggered raging debates.

As the second trial neared, the story had taken on almost mythic proportions.

Court TV brought the entire eight-week trial into living rooms across America. With the gutsiness of *Thelma and Louise* and the vengeance of *Fatal Attraction*, Betty Broderick had captured the imagination, the admiration, and the horror, first of California and then of the nation.

Still no one could quite figure out what had happened to the beautiful, talented, loving mother and wife.

Even after watching the top-rated two-part TV miniseries starring Meredith Baxter, the two-hour *Oprah Winfrey* special, the Barbara Walters *20/20* prison interview, and the *Hard Copy* report, people told me that they didn't understand what had gone on inside her.

For years Betty had accepted everything Dan did without expressing anger. She seemed so passive, so willing to be stepped on that many people couldn't figure out where the intense rage, the use of obscenity, and the lack of control, especially around her children had come from.

In fact it was the repression that finally made the explosion so intense. It also made Betty Broderick controversial and difficult to understand.

Journalists often write what they need to know. I knew there was a more profound story than the ones that had surfaced, and like millions of other people I was hooked. I wrote a proposal and flew out to attend Betty's second trial.

The book that followed is not an investigative examination of Dan and Betty Broderick's struggle. That's what everyone else sought to achieve.

Instead I have tried to get as close as I could to the dark world that she entered, to trace the deterioration and disintegration of her personality and examine the complex forces that brought her there.

This book is not an apology for Betty Broderick and it is not a defense. It is a voyage into the soul of a woman.

PART I

• • •

Till Death
Do Us Part

Darling Dan,

. . . At first it sounds trivial, but when I think about it you are the most important person I have in the whole universe, bar absolutely none. I'd be lost without you. The most significant thing that I discovered in our relationship today is that you are irreplaceable. . . .

But sometimes I feel like I'm speeding along, not seeing what is ahead, anticipating a terrible thing is going to happen to us at any second.

> —*Excerpt from a letter Betty Broderick wrote to Dan on November 5, 1976, exactly thirteen years before she killed him*

November 5, 1989.

Betty opened the back door and walked in. She felt dead and empty inside. She had to make it stop. She had to. She walked up the back stairs in the dark, feeling her way inch by inch, with the gun in her hand.

The door to their bedroom was closed, but the door to the TV room was open. Betty walked in. From the TV room she could see another door that led to the bedroom. It was ajar. She stepped inside, just one step. The drapes were closed, but she could still see them. She was about to say, "Wake up, Dan, I have to talk to you." Then she saw how they were both lying there in the same bed. It was the first time Betty had ever seen them in bed together. She had imagined it a million times with her eyes closed. Almost every time she closed her eyes, she saw them doing it. But this was real. Betty started shaking. The gun was in her hand. Her heart was pounding. She could hardly breathe. It was like a panic attack. Suddenly they moved. Someone yelled, "Call the police." Betty screamed, "No!" She fired the gun. She could hear the noise. She screamed again, and it kept firing. The next thing Betty knew the gun was clicking. She was going to kill herself, but the gun was already empty.

Then Dan sat up. "Okay, you shot me, I'm dead," he moaned as if it were some kind of game they'd been playing all these years and she had just won. He was reaching for the phone on the bedside table. *Oh, no,* she thought. *He's calling the police. He'll put me back in jail.* She pulled the phone out of the wall. The wires got caught. She dropped it and ran.

"I did it. I finally shot the son of a bitch," Betty sobbed into the phone. "The police are gonna be after me. Oh, man, I can't go home. I don't want to scare Danny and Rhett."

"You can come over here, Mom," Lee said as her eyes filled with tears. "Dad doesn't know where I live."

"I'll try, if the cops don't get me on the way over." The phone clicked.

"Oh, God, Jason, wake up," Lee said to her boyfriend. "Mom really did it. She shot Dad."

"She's just saying that. Don't believe her," Jason moaned. "She always says that. Let me sleep. I'm tired."

Betty leaned against the phone booth. Her eyes closed and rolled backwards. Fear gripped the inside of her stomach and spread like an icy hand. She picked up the phone again and dialed. Her voice was so faint that her friend, Dian Black, could hardly hear it. "I shot Dan," Betty whispered, then she dropped the receiver. Dian could hear Betty retching and the receiver dangling on its cord against the wall.

"Where are you? Betty, can you hear me? Where are you?" Dian was practically shouting.

"I don't know," Betty said, coming back. "Someplace off the freeway. Clairmont I think."

Usually Betty was very precise. If asked for directions, she'd list every landmark including the lights and stores on the way and where a meter could be found.

"Read me the number on the phone and stay where you are. I'll have someone call you right back."

Betty gave Dian the number. She hung up, doubled over, and began retching again. She was so dizzy when she heard the phone ringing that she barely managed to reach for the receiver.

"Betty, this is Ronnie Brown. Dian just told me that a tragedy has happened. Where are you, dear? I'll come get you right away."

4

Ronnie's voice was soothing.

"I don't know. Some gas station. I'm near the freeway. There's a Cocoa's Restaurant. I'm going to Lee's if I can get there." The phone went dead. Ronnie stood there numb, listening to the dial tone for half a minute or more, then she threw on a sweat suit and ran outside to her car.

• 3 •

Betty's friend, Brad Wright, was sleeping in the front of the house. He had opened his eyes for a minute when he heard Betty's van start. It was still before daylight. Betty often got up early and drove down to the beach. Brad rolled over and went back to sleep. The next thing he remembered was Danny saying, "Wake up, Brad. There's a phone call for you."

"Betty's been over at Dan's house," Dian Black said, talking very quickly. "Some shots were fired. I'm not really sure what happened. She told me she shot at Dan and Linda."

Ever since he'd started dating Betty, three years earlier, he'd been afraid that this might happen someday, but his immediate concern was whether Dan and Linda were still alive.

It was around seven A.M. Brad threw on his clothes and ran outside, leaving the two sleeping boys alone. He ran across the grass to Gail and Brian Forbes's house. Brian, Dan's law partner, was in the kitchen drinking coffee and reading the newspaper.

"What's wrong?" he asked.

"The worst," Brad answered. "The absolute worst. I think Betty shot Dan and Linda."

"Oh, my God," Brian said. "Let's go. Gail, call the police," he shouted as they ran out the door. "Tell them to meet us there."

Brad drove his Porsche across town like a wild man. He slammed it into the shoulder and jammed on the brakes in front of Dan's house. They both jumped out.

"Turn your emergency flashers on in case the police come. They'll find the place easier," Brian yelled as he ran up the walkway and tried the door. It was locked. Brian slammed on the door with his hand as loudly as he could and yelled for Dan. There was no answer.

"You go that way. I'll go this way," he said to Brad. "Look for an open door or window." Brian was about to put his foot through a window when he saw one ajar on the side of the house where the driveway was. It was about six feet off the ground and it had a screen on it. He ran over and put his fist through the screen, then he ripped it. It was kind of brittle. He was trying to pull the screen off and slide the window up, but he wasn't tall enough. Brad flipped the screen open and pushed the window up. Then Brian climbed through. There was a washer and dryer beneath him. He crawled over them. He got down on the floor and looked around. Brian went diagonally toward the front of Dan's new house looking for bedrooms. He had only been in the place once before and wasn't very familiar with it. He could tell now, by looking, that there were no bedrooms downstairs.

"Dan, Dan," he kept yelling at the top of his lungs from the time he climbed through the window. He thought Dan might be asleep and think someone was breaking in. He didn't know exactly what he was doing except that if they were shot and bleeding, he might be able to help. Brian got to the front of the house where the staircase was. He ran up, past the phone with broken wires, into the bedroom. The first thing he saw was Linda's body. Then he saw Dan's foot.

Linda was lying on top of the bed. Dan was on the floor. They were both greenish.

Brian crouched down and put his hand on Dan's throat. He felt the carotid artery to see if he had a pulse. Dan was cold. Under Dan's face there was a pool of bloody saliva where he had been aspirating blood. He went to Linda and felt the side of her throat. She was cold, too, lying on her stomach spreadeagle with no pulse. The blood was soaking through her white-satin shortie pajamas onto the blue-and-white patchwork quilt.

Brian heard a gasp and looked up. Brad was standing there behind him.

"Go, call someone," Brian managed. "They're both dead."

He stepped back and looked at them for a second longer, then followed Brad. They hit the front door at about the same time on the run, just as two cops, a man and a woman, were coming up the walkway with their guns drawn.

"Call an ambulance," Brian said.

"Stay where you are," the cop yelled.

Oh, no, Brad thought. *They think we did it.*

"Officer," Brian said. "Let me explain."

• 4 •

Up in the bedroom Thomas Valaile checked for a pulse on Dan's neck. He opened one of Dan's eyes to see if there was any tension in it. None. Then he checked Linda. Both bodies were cold.

He walked around the house looking for other victims or suspects that might still be inside. After that he and his partner, Lisa Cook, secured the scene so that no one else could get inside. That was all they could do except to wait for Homicide.

Terrence Degelder, the homicide detective, got there around eight forty-five. It was a clear, warm, cloudless San Diego morning.

He photographed the entire scene, starting from the outside of the house and going all the way to the bedroom. He got pictures of the telephone with its torn wires and a bullet that he found on the rug directly underneath Dan's body. He even photographed the blood he found underneath Dan's face and the bullet he found under Linda's body. Then Degelder photographed the bloody quilt and sheet before he took them as evidence.

There was a hole in the wall of the bedroom. A stray bullet was found between the banisters. Another bullet was embedded in a nightstand eight or nine inches into the wood. Semijacketed lead bullets, .38 caliber. Everything was seized in preparation for the autopsy briefing.

Christopher Swalwell, the deputy medical examiner, found that Linda had two significant gunshot wounds, one in the back of the head, the other in the left upper chest. The bullet in her head had gone through the brain stem. It probably killed her instantly.

Dan had been shot through the lung. Swalwell figured he could have been conscious and moving until the loss of blood and compression on the lung caused him to collapse and become unconscious. It would, he calculated, take at least a couple of minutes to get to that point. It could have been longer, maybe up to half an hour. The blood in Dan's airway indicated that he had lived for a period of time. He had breathed in some of the blood, then aspirated it.

Swalwell knew that Dan had been drinking. He had a blood alcohol level of .04.

Linda, it seemed, had been injured shortly before the killer arrived. She had contusions on the right hand and wrist that were not consistent with injuries caused by fragments from the bullets. They were bleeding right in the skin surface, the kind of thing you'd see from pressure, like someone squeezing the skin or twisting it real hard. Swalwell really didn't have a good explanation for how that had come about. The wound appeared to be fresh, within hours of when she died. That was basically all he could say. It wasn't likely that the intruder had approached her. Whether Dan and Linda had been quarreling before they went to sleep was anyone's guess.

Lee's apartment was warm, but Betty was shivering. Her teeth were chattering. She was pale, crying, and shaking all over. Lee handed her a cup of tea. "Mom," Lee said, "you'll be okay."

The crying in the living room woke Lee's boyfriend. He got up, pushed the hair out of his eyes, and walked toward the bedroom door. A nerve began twitching under his right eye. He had always been on Betty's side. His own father, Frank, had left his mother with a houseful of little kids. He knew firsthand the suffering that it caused. Ever since he met Lee in junior high school, their broken families had been a bond between them.

Betty took one sip of the tea and ran for the bathroom. She looked like she hadn't slept in days.

Lee wanted to call her dad to see if he was all right, but she didn't have the number. Ever since he'd taken her out of his will and kicked her out of the house, she hadn't known how to reach him on his personal line. Dad said it was because of the trouble she'd gotten into, the way she'd screwed up her life. Mom said she was being punished for remaining so close to her.

"I looked at my Holy Card in the kitchen this morning," Betty sobbed, walking out of the bathroom. "It said, 'God will not give you more than you can handle,' but I can't handle this. This is more than I can handle. Why the hell are they doing this to me? Why don't they leave me alone? I can't be reduced to the fines and the threats and the jails again. Why can't they just let me get control of my life and get my kids and have a peaceful, normal life? What the hell do they want? Why did they send me that letter?" Her voice broke. It seemed like a long time before she spoke again.

"It's sadistic what they are doing to me. They've taken everything. There's nothing else left to take. When I read Dan's letter, I started to try to answer it. I was scared Dan was going to put me back in jail, you know. I've tried the lawyers, I've tried the legal system, I can't defend myself, I've exhausted my avenues for coping. I'm turning forty-two in two days. Six years have passed since he started fucking Linda, and it's only gotten worse. God, I was slitting my wrists in 1983, and it's gotten nothing but worse. I can't make this stop. I can't get out of the mess that Dan started."

"I know, Mom," Lee said softly.

"I left the house to go down to the beach. I never got to the beach. First I was just going to go down there to get some air. Then I decided to blow my brains out. But I said, 'No, no. Don't do that. That's not good for the boys. Go over and talk to Dan. Try one more time to talk to Dan.' I was going to ask him for the kids.

"If he wouldn't agree, I was going to kill myself at his house, not down at the beach and not in my house. I was going to splash my brains all over his fucking house so he couldn't say, 'See, I told you she was crazy, I had nothing to do with it.'

"Oh, God, what's going to happen to Danny and Rhett now? I've promised those little boys for years, 'Don't worry, I'll take care of you.' I've disappointed them each time. I promised them that by this September they would be living with me. I promised and I promised. I have been unable to live up to so many promises for so many years. I've absolutely failed those kids." Betty took a deep breath. "I can't get that time with them back. Those moments are gone forever."

Lee looked into her mother's eyes and felt her grief. Betty's lips were thin and colorless. Her brow was furrowed, her gaze intense. The phone rang. Everyone jumped.

"Lee, this is Ronnie Brown. I'm a friend of your mother's. I met her last year at a legal-reform meeting. Your mother called me this morning, dear. I'm at her house with the boys now. Rhett gave me your number. Is she there with you?"

Lee mouthed the name; Betty nodded and took the phone. "Betty," Ronnie said. "I went to the phone booth as fast as I could. I think it was the right one, but you were already gone. I didn't have Lee's address or phone number, so I came here to your house."

Ronnie hesitated. It was difficult to talk with the boys in the next room watching cartoons. She was afraid they might overhear. "Betty," she whispered, "I think you should turn yourself in. My friend Lou knows a lot of lawyers. I'm sure he could help us find

10

someone to give you advice and go with you even though it's Sunday. If there's any chance for leniency, this would be it. Think about it. Call me at home and let me know if you decide you want to do that."

"Okay," Betty said. Her voice was dry and scratchy. "I'll think about it."

"What should I tell the boys?" Ronnie asked.

"Just hug them for me," Betty answered. The words caught in her throat. "Tell them I love them both very much."

• 6 •

The police were crouched behind the bushes watching Rhett ride his bike around the cul-de-sac. When Lee and Jason pulled up in front of Betty's house, they were surrounded almost immediately.

"Hello," Lee said. She could hear her own voice shaking.

"Do you know where your mother is?" the first cop asked.

"She's probably inside," Lee answered, walking past him. "I just came to get my laundry."

She closed the door and ran to the mantel to check the pewter cup for the key to the safe. Betty said it would be there, but it was gone. She grabbed the big burgundy phone book with Betty's initials on the front and threw it in the laundry bag.

"Mommy loves you," Lee said as Rhett followed her out to the car. "Yeah," he said, "I know. What are you trying to tell me?"

"You always were a sharp little kid," Lee answered. "I just think it's going to be our turn to help her."

"Why, what did Mom do? Why are the police here?"

"I don't know yet," Lee answered. Rhett's face wrinkled up like an old lemon. She thought he was about to cry. She hugged him and tried to smile.

"Listen, Rhett, I've gotta go. I'll see you later. Everything's gonna be okay." Jason just stood there next to her, looking depressed.

11

By the time Lee and Jason got back to the apartment, everything was decided. Betty was going to turn herself in. She had talked to Dian and Ronnie. They were going with her. She made plans to meet them in the parking lot of the Magic Pan restaurant. Betty called her father in New York to tell him. She thought it would be easier on him than hearing it from a stranger, but when he said hello, she just couldn't do it.

"Dan's driving me crazy, Daddy. He's driving me up the wall. I feel like killing myself," she said. Then she began sobbing.

"What happened, Elizabeth?" her father asked. Betty had already hung up. The whole call didn't last more than a minute. She caught her breath and dialed her oldest daughter, Kim, who was away at school in Arizona.

"Hi, honey," she said lightly. "I need to tell you something." Then quickly, before she lost her nerve, she said, "I shot Dad this morning. You'd better get on a plane and come home as soon as you can." Lee sat down at the edge of the bed and listened. "Calm down, Kim, just quiet down. Everything will be all right. He was talking. I don't think he's hurt, just come home. Honey, I love you. 'Bye."

Betty walked over to Lee and pulled her up from the bed. She stood back and took Lee's delicate face in her hands. Their eyes met. Betty took off her diamond necklace and her diamond watch. "This stuff is really going to look good on you," she said.

She put the watch on Lee's wrist and clasped the necklace around her long slender neck. Then she handed Lee a check for ten thousand dollars. It was everything she had in her checking account.

"Let's go, honey," she said. "I think it's time."

• 7 •

Dian Black knew what rough divorces were like. At thirty-seven she had already spent fifteen years fighting her ex-husband for child support and custody. Finally she enrolled in legal-aide school and got a job as an arbitrator and clerk for a domestic-law court. At least someone could profit from what she'd learned. Dian even had her own little office above the Jiffy Lube in Pacific Beach.

Now as Dian and Ronnie climbed into the back of Jason's car in University Towne Shopping Centre, there was an awkward silence. It was a strange group to have huddled together in a parking lot in front of the Magic Pan, but the circumstances were even stranger.

"We'll help you, I promise we will," Dian said. She had never seen Betty like this, clear one minute, distant the next. It reminded her of people she'd seen years ago when she worked in a hospital as an aide. People in shock. Betty's body was there with them in Jason's car, but it wasn't Betty. She was trying to go through the motions. She was trying to talk, but a lot of the time she wasn't making any sense.

For a long time Dian had known there were at least two sides to Betty. The happy hostess who looked perfect and never wanted a hair to be out of place. She told the funniest jokes and threw the best parties. The other side was really sad. Dian had always seen the veil of depression. When Betty couldn't fake it, she hid from everyone, wouldn't even answer her telephone.

"We're going to help you," Dian repeated as they drove toward the northern division of the police station. When they got there, even Dian froze. They all sat outside in the car, totally confused about whether to walk in or talk to a lawyer first. Finally they decided that they needed a lawyer. Maybe they should also pick up Betty's personal and legal papers before the police seized them.

It took another half hour to figure out who should get Betty's things and who should call the lawyer. While they were debating, Betty picked up one of Jason's modeling photographs, a headshot, from the floor of the car. She turned it over and scribbled out a will on the back. "If anything happens to me," she told Lee, "I want you four kids to divide up whatever is left."

The news came on the radio. "Prominent attorney Dan Broderick and his wife, Linda, have been shot," the announcer said. "An all-out search for his estranged wife, Betty Broderick, has begun."

13

"Oh, God, they're closing in on us," Betty said. "We'd better hurry."

Dian ran to get her car. Ronnie and Betty rushed over to a phone booth to call Ron Frantz, the first lawyer on their list. Jason held Lee's hand and stepped on the gas.

• 8 •

Lee had forgotten the key. Jason boosted her up. She broke a window, climbed in, then ran and opened the door. They found a whole box of stuff under Betty's desk. She started looking through it. Then she got nervous.

"Let's get out of here," Lee said, picking up the box. They threw it in the back of Jason's car. She wanted to make it back to the phone booth so that Betty could take the papers to the lawyer. In the rear-view mirror she suddenly saw the cop cars with their red-and-blue lights flashing.

"Oh, shit," Jason moaned, "we're surrounded."

A tall guy in uniform came walking toward the car with his hand on his gun. Lee's feet began tapping nervously against the floor mat. Her legs were shaking. She thought the cops were going to take the diary and the papers. The cop opened the car door and gestured. Jason and Lee were put in back of the police car and driven to a parking lot in Pacific Beach. It was swarming with cops. They took Lee and put her in one car, then they put Jason in another.

"Mom was at my house," Lee admitted when they got to the station, "but she left when someone honked for her outside. I didn't see who she went with or where she went." Lee told the cop about the big brown leather pocketbook with the brass trim and the gun that her mother had been carrying. She had to give them something.

"It's still back at the apartment on the table next to my bed if you

14

want to see it," Lee said. She wanted to tell the truth, but she also wanted to protect her mother, Jason, Ronnie, and Dian. It was a tough balancing act. "Mom told me that she shot at Dan and Linda, but it was dark, and the drapes were drawn. She didn't know if she hit anyone."

"Lee," the police officer said, "your father and Linda are both dead."

Lee sat perfectly still. Her body felt overwhelmingly heavy. She had a sudden sense of the horror that lay ahead. Danny and Rhett would have to be told. They'd be like orphans. They were so young. What would they do without a dad or a mom? A lot of memories passed before her: her father's refusal to let Mom have custody or visitation; Danny and Rhett on Mom's answering machine crying for her; the school calling to say the boys had been coming to school hungry and with colds and holes in their shoes. Only now did she realize how much things like that had tortured her mother. She remembered her father asking if her mom had a gun. "Mom," she said, "Dad thinks you have a gun." Betty went into the bedroom and closed the door, then came out carrying the gun. Lee saw it again in the pocket of Betty's robe one morning when Dan came over to pick her up.

Lee looked at the cop and wiped her eyes. "Before they separated, before Linda came along, we always had a happy family," she said. "They had a lot of friends. They didn't fight much. When they did, they went into the bedroom so we wouldn't hear. Over the years Mom changed, but I was so close to it that I couldn't really see all the changes that much."

The detective nodded sympathetically. "Go on," he said.

"Mom was always good to us. That part never changed. When we were around her, she would try to hold back her tears. Anger was easier for her than pain. Sometimes I think it was the anger that got my mother up in the morning."

Looking back, there had been so many warnings, so many terrifying changes. But there were still a lot of times when Betty seemed like her old happy-go-lucky self, the classic, perfect suburban mother who drove the Chevy van with the LODEMUP license plates and got up at six A.M. on Sunday mornings to put worms on the boy's fishing hooks.

15

She even laughed about breaking both wrists roller-skating with her kids.

"God," Lee said, "maybe it was all my fault. Maybe if I'd taken her, seriously and listened to her, I could have prevented this. But how could I believe that my mom would kill my dad? Everybody else just gets divorced." Now she'd never make up with Dad. They'd never have a chance to say good-bye. Things had just started to get a little bit better between them. They'd gone out to dinner for her eighteenth birthday. He was glad she'd straightened out and gotten her GED. But it was too late. She'd never had a chance to say she was sorry that she disappointed him. Sorry that she'd experimented with cocaine and left school after the ninth grade. She'd never be able to tell him that she was going to make something of her life. Now she couldn't even let him know that she really loved him.

• 9 •

"What are your assets, Mrs. Broderick?" Ron Frant asked.

"I don't know," Betty answered. "I never know how much money I have. I never know."

"Well," he said, "how about your kids' insurance policies?"

"I won't touch them," she answered. "I have no idea if I can pay you or not."

"Then I can't handle your defense," he said. "I'll walk you into the police station. I'll make sure your legal rights are respected and you're treated fairly. After that you're on your own."

Ron Frant spent several hours with Betty, then came out and told Dian and Ronnie to keep Betty hidden while he made some arrangements. He didn't want her arrested in his office. Dian's car had tinted windows, so they drove around with Betty for about half an hour. When they got tired of that, they parked in front of Anthony's Seafood place to wait. Ron pulled up a few minutes later. Betty smiled politely and kissed Ronnie and Dian good-bye. Then she doubled over, and the dry heaves began again.

As soon as she could stand up, Ron Frant walked her in. He knew all the cops. He'd called ahead of time and made a deal. "I'm bringing Broderick in," he'd said, "but you're not to ask her a single thing."

Keeping quiet wasn't easy for Betty. She wanted to tell them absolutely everything. "I have nothing to hide," she told Frant. Still he forbade it. "Remember," Frant reminded her when they walked through the door, "not a word." Betty nodded. She was so quiet, she didn't even say hello.

By evening they had her all locked up in a small padded suicide cell in Las Calinas Prison. She was stark naked. It was the practice with suicide risks because they might use their clothes to hang themselves.

Curled up in a fetal position on a small bare cot, Betty Broderick finally slept. She felt safe now for the first time in six years. At last she believed that Daniel Broderick, the only man she had ever loved, couldn't hurt her anymore.

PART II

•••

The
Early Years

"It seems so foolish to admit this now, but the instant I saw him, it was like a lightning bolt. That sudden and that intense that I fell in love with him. . . . It never happened to me before and it never happened to me since . . . but that's the way it was."

—Betty Broderick describing her first date with Dan Broderick

Daniel Broderick was the oldest son born to a large Irish Catholic family in Pittsburgh. His father, the first Broderick to attend college, graduated from Notre Dame and became a naval officer and lumber wholesaler.

"Yolanda," he would call from upstairs in a thundering voice. Then, he'd ring a bell. That meant he was about to come down to eat. Yolanda stopped whatever she was doing and began carrying his food to the table. Every piece of toast was arranged just perfectly. When the old man entered the dining room, the kids fell silent. No one talked when he was eating dinner.

Yolanda was pregnant every year, so there were nine kids to keep quiet—she had no education and no job. Once Betty asked, "Why don't you leave him?"

"And go where?" Yolanda answered.

Sometimes it seemed to Betty that Yolanda didn't feel worthy to be the rug he stomped on. None of the girls in that family did. They did the laundry and the cleaning. They waited on Dad and the boys.

The old man disciplined all of them hard. He also expected a lot of them. Every one of those boys went to Notre Dame, but Dan was considered the brightest. He was focused, charming, handsome, and driven, a role model for the others, a brilliant, aggressive kid who drank hard but always seemed to be on the right path. Drinking was a Broderick family tradition. Even Yolanda took comfort in a few hard drinks before dinner.

Betty Bisceglia was the third of six children. Her father, Frank, was the youngest in a large Italian family of plasterers and bricklayers. He was a quiet little man with sparkling blue eyes who lived and died for his wife and children. Family was everything to him, always had been. He owned and operated a successful construction company. He sent all of his children to Catholic school. Frank was a hands-on father, active in the local church, the Knights of Columbus, and the PTA. He even drove the kids to dancing lessons, did the shopping, and fixed his wife's coffee each morning. But Marita ran the house. She was a tall, aristocratic woman who had grown up on art books and dancing lessons. She and her sister were among a select few women of her day who had college educations. Marita was a great cook and a great hostess.

Marita had been a schoolteacher, so it was assumed that all the children would do well in school. Some people said she was a snob because her kids always had to have the best of everything, good jewelry for the girls, real jewelry. The right purses, the right leather gloves, the right shoes that matched, and matched sets of luggage. They looked great, not overdone, long hemlines and sashes, nothing obvious. Hermès scarves, suede skirts, everything understated. At thirteen Betty was modeling at Bonwit Teller.

Betty didn't even realize how lucky she was, because the whole little society she lived in was like that. The girls knew about linens and jewelry and art and silver, not because their mother said, "Now I'm going to teach you," but just because that was the way they lived and entertained. There were strict social rules too. Marita was extremely strict about whom Betty could date.

Marita didn't drive, so Frank did the errands. He was there for them on the weekends and in the evenings. Betty had a mother and a father, and they had each other. Her father made enough money for everything they needed, but they never talked about how much he made. The Cape Cod house in the small town of Eastchester reflected their love more than their money. It was a cheerful, traditional home filled with the belief that marriage was forever. Each of the kids had jobs. Everyone did chores around the house. They were all very religious, very smart, and very high achievers.

Betty was the golden girl, with long blond hair, her father's blue eyes, and her mother's long legs, perfect teeth, and aristocratic features. Underneath, Betty was always a mystery, filled with contradictions, smart, ambitious, funny, and at the same time timid and insecure.

Betty always took care of little kids, wounded birds, stray dogs and cats, anything that seemed lost. Even as a young child she could be found carrying a baby on her hip or an animal in her arms and caring for it while keeping up a lively patter of conversation.

Betty went from the Immaculate Conception grammar school to a Catholic all-girls high school in Hartsdale, New York. She participated in Girl Scouts, horseback riding, tennis, riflery, waterskiing, and golf. Somehow she got straight A's and worked two jobs at the same time.

She had lots of friends, but stayed very reserved when it came to boys. She didn't like the necking that started in the sixth grade. All those tall, skinny boys with pimples wanted to go on dates, but she wouldn't go. She knew all they would do was end up at the movies and neck. If she wanted to spend time with someone, she wanted to talk to him. She wanted to get to know him.

At seventeen she enrolled at Mount Saint Vincent's College for Girls in Riverdale, New York. She had just been in college for a few weeks when her friend's brother invited her to a chaperoned football weekend at Notre Dame. Since it was an all-boys Catholic school in South Bend, Indiana, her mother said yes. Calls were exchanged between parents. Betty traveled with another girl and stayed in an old lady's house. The campus was beautiful. The boy, Bill Shields, was attentive. One of the activities during the weekend was a senior class party. Jerry Lee Lewis was performing. It was crowded, noisy, and a great adventure for a girl whose only parties had been at an all-girls high school gym. Betty was sitting at a table across from a young man who asked if she had a pen. She gave him one. He grinned at her and wrote Daniel Broderick across the tablecloth. After it he put the initials, M.D.(A.). Betty fell for the bait.

"What's the *A* for?" she asked.

"For almost," he answered, smiling. "I've just been accepted to Cornell Medical School in New York, and I'm celebrating."

"Oh, I'm from New York," Betty said cheerfully.

"Can I look you up when I get there?" he asked.

"Sure," she answered politely. "I'll show you around." Knowing how far Cornell was from the part of New York where she lived, Betty figured it was just party talk. She gave him her name and address, but never expected to see him again. Dan had different ideas. She didn't know it at the time, but after she left, he turned to his friend.

"See that girl? I'm going to marry her," he said.

Several weeks later she got her first telegram with a mysterious message. Another telegram followed, then phone calls and letters. Dan had been planning to attend a football game in New York and wanted to surprise Betty, but the plans didn't work out. They began writing long letters and sending funny cards and notes back and forth. Betty loved getting them. She received at least one long letter from Dan every single day, always signed "Love, D" with an *X* for a kiss. She answered them during boring class lectures.

When Dan came to New York to begin school, they had agreed to meet under the clock at the Biltmore Hotel at Grand Central Station. The day came. Betty felt very shy, not sure he would really be there. She wasn't used to traveling to Manhattan alone. She had only met him once over a year before. She wasn't even sure she'd recognize him. She recalled that he was shorter than her own five feet eleven inches. When he called and said, "I was there. Where were you?" she apologized and promised to meet him on Friday at his dorm after class.

"I'm going downtown because I promised this guy I would meet him," she told a friend, "but he's too short for me. After today I'll fix you up with him, and I'll go out with a friend of his."

Betty got there early and waited in the lobby for Dan to show up. When she saw him in the crowd of white-lab-coated students, it felt like an electric current had just passed through her body. It left her trembling and weak. It was the strangest feeling. She couldn't believe it. She didn't really know what it was.

Wow, she said to herself. *It must be love.*

Right from the beginning Dan needed to lead. He was even resentful when she made plans to show him around New York. She'd lived there all her life. She was the one with the friends. She knew the city. On their third date he was driving her car around New York. She suggested visiting her friends at Mount Saint Vincent's. He pulled over to the side of the road.

24

"Let's just get one thing straight," he yelled. "You don't tell me what we're going to do."

"Okay," Betty answered, surprised and hurt. "What do you want to do?"

He looked at her. There was fury in his eyes. "Nothing special," he snapped. "But you don't make the decisions, I do. That's my job."

"Sure," Betty said lightly, but she felt shaken. She wondered if she really wanted to spend all her time with Dan. Even when he wasn't angry, he was very controlling and very possessive. Dan hung around New York all summer instead of going to his family's beach house, just so she wouldn't date anyone else.

The one Christmas he went home, he heard she had a date with someone else on New Year's Eve and flew back so that she couldn't go. Betty was still on home turf. If he treated her badly, she could just make him get out of her sports car and go home.

Most of the time he treated her like a prize he hoped to win, falling all over her. He said that all his life he had literally dreamt of meeting someone like her. He had pictures taken of her just so he could show people how beautiful she was when they were apart. For three years he begged her to marry him. Every day he told her he loved her.

On weekends they drove up to the mountains in her little MG and went skiing. At times like that he really opened up to her. She felt so close to him that they almost seemed like one person. She knew his thoughts before he said them. She knew his dreams, his aspirations, his soul. She knew what drove him.

Compared with Betty, Dan was a geek. He wasn't brought up in a suburban New York household as she was. He didn't know about things she knew about. And even though he dressed well, it was always a little too much—not understated like Betty.

For her nineteenth birthday Dan gave her a large, framed, color portrait of himself. The girls at school thought it was very funny. Apparently Dan figured it was just what she had always wanted. In a way he was right.

Betty was part of a generation of girls who grew up believing that someday her prince would come. That was the fairy tale. The dream of her generation. Even strong, smart, energetic girls like Betty were taught to stand behind someone else they were supposed to think of as stronger. It was the little game their mothers had always played regardless of who was really in charge. Everything about the way Betty was raised taught her that someday she would become part of someone else. In exchange for this fusion of identity she would be supported, nurtured, and loved. Dan Broderick was exactly the kind of man she was raised to marry.

When he took Betty home to Pittsburgh to meet his family, his sisters thought she was Grace Kelly. She was a trophy, a classy, great-looking girl. Her friends couldn't believe she was marrying him. He wasn't blonde, blue-eyed, athletic, or rich.

"Yes," she said. "He's short and dark, but he's smart and funny, and if a guy isn't smart and funny, I can't have anything to do with him."

To Betty it seemed like the perfect match. The were both intelligent and ambitious. They were the same religion, and they both wanted the same things in life—wealth, status, and a large family.

For their engagement Dan planned dinner at a Japanese restaurant. He gave her a beautiful ring. After he gave it to her, he got so drunk, she practically had to carry him home.

Betty wanted to finish school before getting married, so she raced ahead and graduated half a year early. Underneath she knew that her education was really a joke. Nursing and teaching were acceptable until you became a mother or while you were supporting your husband, but they were not to be taken seriously. Serious work was the man's job. She still wanted the degree and to experience teaching.

Betty lucked out. Home for a visit, she walked into the Ann Hutchinson School, which had just been built on the dirt lot that used to be across from her house. She figured she'd pick up an application. There were tarpaulins all over the place and ladders. They were painting. Betty walked up to a man with gray hair and a plaid shirt. She thought he was a painter.

"I'm looking for a job. Do you know where I can pick up an application?" It turned out that he was the superintendent. She never would have met him if she'd gone for a regular interview. They started talking. In an hour she had a job. He never asked for a résumé. She didn't even fill out an application.

"One of my third-grade teachers has cancer and can't come back. How would you like to start the Monday after Christmas?" he said.

She was twenty-one with platinum-blond hair, huge blue eyes, and long legs shown to advantage in the days of the miniskirt. Betty couldn't help thinking that being young and pretty had helped her land the job.

The kids loved her. They never wanted to go home. The parents loved her. The principal would come to her and ask about all the families. This was her neighborhood. These were her people.

Betty was thrilled beyond belief. She loved the work; the money was great. She had paid off her car. She was still living at home with a maid to do the laundry and cooking and a closetful of beautiful, expensive clothes. Best of all she had a handsome boyfriend in medical school who couldn't wait to marry her.

• 2 •

Betty had waited all her life for this day. So had her mother. The wedding was scheduled for April 1969, in the Immaculate Conception Church near her parents' house. Marita had her own ideas about how things should go. She and Dan were both used to controlling Betty. In the end they did it Dan's way and rented a white Rolls-Royce. Dan also refused the cutaway tuxedo Marita wanted him to wear. He chose his own custom-made double-breasted, blue pinstripe and flowered tie. Betty was wrapped in delicate and exquisite lace. Dan showed up with a hangover. He never even told her she looked pretty, having started on the champagne right away. He was staggering around stepping on the train of her dress all through the wedding.

"I'm going to throw up," he said when they got up to the altar.

"If you throw up, I'm going to die," she whispered back.

He was still drunk when they got on the plane to Saint Thomas. It was so hot and humid there that Betty could feel her hair curl as soon as they stepped outside. They had to find a cab and deal with all the suitcases. They were exhausted when they finally got to the villa.

Betty was all dressed up. Very Jackie Kennedy, a lemon-yellow wool coat over a matching dress. The top of the dress was plain lemon yellow like the coat. The matching skirt was gray, white, and yellow. The outfit had little pockets, white buttons, and a Peter Pan collar. She even had on a matching yellow bra. Betty figured she'd take a shower and put on her new Lord & Taylor silky satin white negligee with the blue ribbon. Maybe they'd take a nap first. She wasn't sure. She never spent a lot of time fantasizing about exactly how it would go, just thought it would be very romantic.

She got raped in that prim outfit. His pants were still on. So was her dress. She was his wife now. He could do anything he wanted to do. Their suitcases were still unopened at the foot of the bed. He threw her on her back, unzipped his pants, pulled up her skirt, and wham. Very businesslike, no foreplay at all. The whole thing was over in five minutes, and nothing after either. He was drunk. He just kind of passed out.

Betty lay there stunned and crying. She didn't know what to do. She had no frame of reference, but she still knew that this wasn't how it was supposed to be. She didn't want him to think she was frigid or a prude, but she was hurt and disappointed. All her life she'd been thinking about this moment. Long before she knew who, how, or when, she thought that on her wedding night she would become one with him and that all her dreams would come true. Her husband would sweep her up in his arms and make love to her.

Dan must have known she was disappointed, but she never told him. She didn't want to hurt his feelings. If he wanted to be the ape-man, then she'd let him. She was willing. She just hadn't expected it of him.

The next morning he was really in a black mood. He let the maids go and walked around sulking. She was supposed to cook. So she did lunch. He ate it without talking. Then she had to wash the dishes and do the laundry and the sheets.

"Let's go to Saint Thomas and go shopping," she suggested cheerfully. Dan didn't want to go. He wouldn't go.

"Hey," she said, really feeling hurt. "This is our honeymoon. Aren't we trying to do something together?"

He brought out a stack of books and sat by the pool reading them.

"Put on your bathing suit," he said, finally looking up from his books. "I want to take some pictures of you." He took a lot of pictures of her looking skinny in a little two-piece bathing suit.

"You're really hot stuff," he said.

<h1 style="text-align:center">• 3 •</h1>

Betty moved into his cubicle and shared the tiny bathroom with Dan and his roommate. It would be summer before a married-students' room was available. Now she had to commute everyday from Manhattan to work in Eastchester. There was no living space and even less storage space for her clothes, which she had divided into separate seasons. She had to forget about her records, tapes, books, mementos, and other things.

Still, Betty bounced back. She had fun a lot of the time. They lived at Sixty-ninth and York, near the heart of a good section of Manhattan. They'd go to all the great New York bars; they'd go to museums. During vacations they rode horses and water-skied and snow skied. When Dan was elected the social chairman of Cornell Medical School, she practically ran a dating service. The medical students didn't know anybody. She'd invite her entire alma mater to these parties. Dan was very proud of her when she put on parties for the whole medical school.

During spring break and summer vacation they would sometimes visit friends. Dan presented Betty like a prize. When an old classmate from Notre Dame came to see him at medical school, Dan said, "I gotta see his face when he sees it's you. He was there the first night we met, and I told him I was going to marry you."

A few weeks later Betty got sick, nauseated and vomiting up all the time. "I'm sorry, I'm sorry. I never get sick. I'm sure I'll be better soon," she kept saying.

Dan grinned. "Don't worry, you're not damaged goods," he said. "You're pregnant."

"Pregnant," she gasped. She'd had a lifetime of Catholic training about how to be a wife, but sex and birth control had never been mentioned.

"I love children," Betty said. "I want nine or ten, but not now. I didn't expect to have a baby so soon. I expected to teach and to entertain. I thought you'd go to school and I'd work. We'd go to Europe together and dress very well. We'd enjoy New York. I want to work and travel and entertain, not raise a baby in a dorm room in New York City."

Betty went to a doctor and asked about a D and C. "Don't worry. You'll never carry this child to term. You have two uteruses," he told her. He was wrong. She taught through the term, violently ill all the time. In June she was still sick and still pregnant. The last day of school was a tremendous relief. She couldn't hold anything down. All she wanted to do was collapse, but they needed money, so she took a summer job selling nurses' uniforms and supplies in the medical center. She kept throwing up before, after, and during work.

"If I quit," she said, "I'll just be lying around sick all day in an un-air-conditioned cubicle." In September she went back to teaching. She concealed her pregnancy till Christmas by wearing big clothes and tight girdles. Betty planned to quit at the end of January and take February off. On January 24th she went into labor. Dan had been drinking all day with another student named Daniel Boone. He showed up with Boone on one arm and someone she thought was a high-class hooker in a mink coat on the other.

"Dan, I'm in labor," Betty moaned.

"Well, okay, how about fixing a drink for me and my friends," he said.

For months Betty had been making excuses about the drinking. He worked hard, he studied hard, he played hard, he drank hard, she told herself. All through college he'd been a very heavy drinker. He had passed out, got into accidents, got into fights. She didn't hate him for it; she felt sorry for him. She assumed it was because he was so pressured. Alcohol seemed to be his only release. That night Betty couldn't forgive him. "Dan," she said again. "I'm going to have the baby." He just kept grinning at the hooker. She began to cry. "The hell with this," she decided, feeling angry and hurt. "I'll go to the hospital without you."

"Hey," he said. "Wait a minute. Okay, I'll take you." He stumbled after her. He passed out in the hallway. By the time he woke up, Betty had not only taken a cab to the hospital, but she had given birth to a baby girl.

Nothing was ready. Not a diaper or a sheet or a shirt or a bed. They put Kim in a drawer lined with a blanket. Marita had a few essentials delivered from Saks. Betty returned the wedding gifts she hadn't already used and got credit for the baby. Her friends planned an emergency baby shower. She walked in carrying Kim. Betty never went back to finish the school year. She was completely committed to the idea of a mother's staying home for the first two or three years.

Kim was very good and very beautiful, but Betty felt alone. The feeling stretched back even before the aloneness she felt with Dan, back to Catholic school, back to the house in Eastchester, back to the lifetime of longing for the events that were supposed to complete her.

Betty threw herself more deeply into the marriage commitment. Commitment replaced joy. She took a job in an apartment building a block away baby-sitting a seven-month-old. The baby's mother was a law student, the father was a research assistant at NYU. Since they were day students, it was a full-time job. At least she and the baby were out of the dorm. She also began trying to sell Avon and Tupperware. It wasn't very profitable. Everyone in the neighborhood was as poor as they were. If she was lucky, she'd end up standing there outside someone's door with the baby in one arm and the Tupperware samples in the other. Usually she couldn't even get that far because the buildings had security systems. Betty had gotten so lonely that she welcomed any excuse to talk to people.

At twenty-one, married less than a year, she felt used up and powerless. Dan had won his trophy and put her at home on the shelf. He didn't have to train anymore. "God, Dan. I'd love to do what you're doing," she said. "It would be great just to sit in on some of your classes." He lifted his eyes from a book. "I've begun to consider options for a medical specialty," he said. "I want one that would definitely make me rich, a millon a year before I turn forty. That's the bottom line, the main reason I chose medicine in the first place."

Betty nodded. "I know. Your dreams are grandiose. All I want is a microwave oven."

"I think I could make a million a year faster if I went to law school after medical school," Dan said the next night. "There's a whole new industry of medical malpractice starting up. If I become a doctor and a lawyer, I can start at the top."

"If that's what you want to do, I'll back you one hundred percent," Betty told him. "You're better suited to law than to medicine. Besides, I'll vote for being rich any day."

His dream was hers. She was the handmaiden, aiding and abetting his life. She would take care of his house, be a hostess for his parties, and raise his children. He would make enough money to take care of them in style. That was the deal. Dan believed everything else to do with family was women's work.

Later that year Dan was admitted to the University of Virginia, Stanford, and Harvard law schools. He could have gone to law school at night or part-time while earning money. He could have gone to a state school with low tuition. Betty wanted a warmer climate. Harvard was very expensive and didn't have a part-time program or a warm climate. "But you can't say no to Harvard," Dan explained.

"I guess you're right," Betty answered, smiling.

They moved to Pittsburgh for the summer and lived in his parents' house along with Dan's unmarried brothers and sisters because it was free. Dan began an internship at a local hospital. Thirty-six hours on, twelve hours off. Betty never saw him. During Kim's afternoon naps she tried to sell Tupperware in the hills of Pittsburgh, but there wasn't enough free time even to earn spending money. She ended up borrowing from Dan's mother and feeling like a leech.

In August they moved to Cambridge. It was the fourth move in sixteen months. Living on loans and Betty's small income, they couldn't even afford the student housing. Dan went ahead to choose the apartment. "I found a great place in Somerville with a yard for Kim," he said.

It was a basement apartment. The windows looked out on deep concrete wells. Every morning the wells were filled with liquor bottles and beer cans. No one in the neighborhood spoke English. It was a Portuguese factory district. The mothers went to work and left the babies with grandmothers. Betty's dream of re-creating the best of her own childhood for Kim was ruined. She wanted a real home. Safe and warm and secure. Most of the winter the heat and hot water didn't work. Some nights it was so cold, she thought the baby would be dead by morning. She practically lay on top of Kim to keep her warm. She had to heat water just to give the baby a bath or to wash her own hair. They had no car. Dan said they didn't need one because he had a motorcycle. Betty worked every day minding a law student's baby and had a part-time night job at Lord & Taylor. When Dan came home, Betty went to work. On the nights she didn't have to work, she'd load up the wash and take a bus to the Laundromat. They were so poor that they couldn't have made it without the government-surplus food.

She was carrying the diapers, the laundry, and the surplus food home on the bus one night when she began to feel nauseated. Once again Betty was pregnant. Once again Dan said he really wanted the baby. Betty was sick the whole pregnancy. Her vision got blurry, she developed horrible vascular problems. This time it was even impossible to lie down for a nap. Whenever she tried to sleep, Kim cried. "So this is marriage," Betty thought. "This is the dream I was waiting for. It changed my life all right. In eighteen months I've gone from independence and money to poverty and helplessness. My needs are always second to Dan's and the baby's. I'm always losing."

33

They never went out. There was no money for a baby-sitter or clothes.

Dan refused help from his parents. But somehow there was always enough for what he wanted. He went on ski trips and bought fancy clothes. She tried to convince herself that he needed these things and deserved them since he was working so hard to build a life for the family. Whenever her anger and jealousy surfaced, she tried to control it.

More and more Betty envied his life at Harvard. He never shared it with her. When he finally came home, usually late at night, he was too busy studying or too drunk to talk about anything. She began to think about divorce. The night she came home and found him drunk and hitting Kim, she decided to leave. She actually packed up and did it. "This is it," she told him, her voice shaking with fear and rage. "I've had it with you. You're sick. I want a divorce."

A few days later she came back. Where could she go with a baby on one hip and another on the way? Besides, the dream of her entire life was to marry a hardworking man so that he could take care of her and the children while she took care of him. She almost had that, if she could just hold on. Her own career no longer mattered. She worked so many night jobs and weekend jobs, she could hardly remember which was which. Slowly things began to improve, just as she told herself they would.

• 4 •

Betty Broderick on Her Early Years with Dan

"When Dan was in his first year of law school, he beat Kim up because she wouldn't be quiet. We had a pullout sofa bed. He was on the sofa bed, hitting her. I was working at a Jolly Roger restaurant. When I came home, I freaked out. I told him he was a dangerous and troubled person. I couldn't believe it. He had this look in his eye, and that's what scared me. Dan drank a lot in those years. I didn't know what to do, so I left. I packed up and left. I went on a Greyhound bus to my parents'. I said I was never coming back. I went to New York, but when I got to New York, I couldn't tell my parents why I had come. I just pretended I went to have a visit.

"I didn't want to tell them. I just didn't. I felt too ashamed. I was already pregnant with my second child. Besides, they wouldn't have taken me in. They believed that once you were married, you made it work no matter what. They had just given me a big wedding. They would have been too embarrassed. I stayed in New York quite a while, I don't remember how long. I had no money. That bus ride cost about eighteen dollars from Boston to New York. I barely had the eighteen dollars.

"Kim had this little sack of clothes from my mother, and on this bus ride she wanted to crawl on this filthy bus. She was so dirty when we got to New York, the kid had never been so dirty. It was the longest ride of my life. But when I got there, I felt safe. I was home. I had a bedroom. And I had Kim. My mom and dad were happy to see me. Dan cried and cried. He always cried and begged like that after he was mean. He promised me that he would never, ever ever touch the baby again, ever. So I finally went back. He never hit her after that. He washed somebody's mouth out with soap once, which I didn't approve of. Dan made a big deal out of his father twisting ears and pulling hair and pinching and dragging and kicking. He made a big deal out of his father hurting him, and I made it real clear that you're not hurting our kids. This was a ten-month-old baby. What could she do wrong?

"Later, when he had custody and I was no longer there, Rhett and Danny were telling me that he was kicking them, throwing them across rooms, choking them, hurting them, and this was what he said his father did to him. Now, he didn't do it to the girls, because the girls were older, teenagers. He psychologically hurt those girls by telling them they weren't pretty enough. That they weren't skinny enough. That they didn't have blond hair and blue eyes and they were dumb. That's the way a Broderick man gets at a woman. So he was considering the girls more as women than children. But children and little dogs he could kick and punch.

"The boys misbehaved in a restaurant one night, and I think that's the time he choked Rhett, held him up against a brick wall and choked him because the children were kicking each other under the table in a restaurant.

"While we were still together, he smashed the fish tank, he smashed the chair, he smashed cars, and a few times he smashed me. But as long as he didn't hit the kids, I made light of it.

"They didn't know that he drank in those days. The kids went to bed at seven or eight o'clock. He wouldn't be home at seven or eight o'clock. It was between eleven and four in the morning when he came home. What my kids did know was that I had to go get him out of jail once for drinking and driving. And I had to wake up four sleeping children because I couldn't leave them alone and I didn't have a live-in maid. We had a Colt station wagon at the time. I had to carry them in the middle of the night downstairs to the car, sound asleep, to go down to the jail in San Diego to get him out.

"I don't know how the boys handle the stuff that they hear about me now from the Broderick family, but actually they experienced Dan and Linda firsthand. I didn't have to tell them what was going on. Everyone shows their true colors, everyone does. You can play a good game with some of the people some of the time, but you're basically always yourself. The better you know people, the more the initial stuff wears off and the real stuff is there. Now that it's all behind us, I hope they still know how much I love them."

• 5 •

Dan's grandmother felt sorry for them and bought them an old Volkswagen. It was a lifesaver. They could finally move out of the inner city to the suburbs. Now Kim had children to play with. Betty started doing day care again. She had other mothers to talk to. They bought a secondhand bedroom set and a used Portacrib. This time at least she'd be ready for the new baby when it came. Dan was studying the night she went into labor. "It's an important test," he said. "How about taking a cab to the hospital?" She was hurt, but she did it.

Lee was a wonderful baby, and Betty was deeply committed to being the perfect mother and wife no matter how Dan acted. During the day she took care of her own babies and did the day care to earn extra money. At night she prepared big meals for him. She tried to please Dan and to keep out of his way. It was a delicate balancing act, not dissimilar to what her mother-in-law, Yolanda, had done.

Dan landed a summer clerkship in L.A. They couldn't afford to keep the apartment in Boston, so they packed everything they could fit into the Volkswagen and drove across the country. With both babies strapped into car seats, five days seemed like five weeks.

L.A. was warm and lively, but very crowded and not as beautiful as Betty had hoped. One Saturday they drove south on Interstate 5. They ended up in the Mission Bay area of San Diego. Betty walked around. "Now, this is beautiful," she said. Across the clear, sparkling water she could see the skyline of San Diego. "They must have law firms here," Dan said. He looked at the miles and miles of Pacific coastline. He saw the joggers, bicyclists, and Windsurfers. Just like that, right then and there, Dan decided that San Diego was where they would live. Betty was thrilled.

The new plan was enough to sustain her all summer. There was only one problem. She was pregnant with a third child. "Enough is enough." She told Dan, "My body is not under my control anymore, and it's supposed to be. I know what another pregnancy will be like. I know what caring for another baby would mean, and I don't want to do it. I don't want the sleepless nights and the howling, and the Laundromats." Dan's face fell.

"Kim's not even three, and Lee's just an infant. I can't do what's right for them. If I'm pregnant, I'll be throwing up again. I'll be tired and anemic with varicose veins. I'll be trying to do everything with both kids. I'll still be working and cooking and you'll never be home or help me. Abortion is legal in New York. I want one. I'm only a few weeks pregnant."

They drove to New York. When they got to the clinic, Dan started crying. "I promise this time I'll help. I'll be home more," he said. "I'll be better to you and the kids."

"You want it that much?" she asked. Dan nodded. She kissed him and dried his eyes with her tissue.

"Oh, God, Dan. I love you so much," she said.

They turned around and headed home. This time she wasn't only sick, she bled through the entire pregnancy. The doctors called it placenta previa.

Dan didn't help at all. Instead he joined the student council. Now he had extracurricular activities and a busier life than ever. When she went into labor, he was away in Vermont on a ski trip with some old college friends. "There's not enough money for you to go," he said. "Anyhow, in your condition you can't ski, so why bother?"

The baby was six weeks early again. Betty was hemorrhaging so much that she was taken to the hospital in a police car. A neighbor minded the girls. There was a snowstorm and her doctor couldn't get there. The doctor filling in for him didn't realize the baby was breach.

He left her alone in the room. The baby was born with no one to help. It died a day and a half later.

Dan came home from the ski trip and arranged for everything. Relatives arrived. The baby was cremated. It was a lovely service.

"I'm fine," Betty assured everyone, still repressing her anger and her grief. When they left, Dan walked into the bathroom and found her. She had swallowed all the pills in the medicine cabinet.

• 6 •

The move to San Diego brought her back. Dan was constantly giving instructions. He kept her on eggshells all the time. In some ways it was helpful. She was so busy trying to please him, there was no time to think. There was packing to do, furniture to be sold, neighbors to say good-bye to. They had finally made it. All the sacrifices had paid off. Dan was a full-fledged doctor and a Harvard-trained lawyer. He'd been hired by Gray Cary, Ames and Frye, the best law firm in San Diego.

"I told you it would be worth it. I told you if you gave me the time, I'd give you and the kids everything you always wanted. In another year or two we'll be there."

They found a scrungy little apartment in the Plumtree Complex, in Sierra Mesa, near the stadium. It was across from the laundry room. The units had their own playground and swimming pool. Right down the road was a Catholic church and the Columbia Catholic grammar school. Betty got a part-time job teaching fifth grade in the afternoons. She didn't have to be there until after lunch. She could put the kids down for their naps, then earn the extra money. She could even walk over. Betty found a neighbor to baby-sit who needed money.

Then in September, on the way to her first faculty meeting, she got violently ill again. "Oh, my God," she thought. "I've just lived through a year of being sick and the death of the baby. I know what will happen if I tell Dan. I can see the look on his face.

"I'm tired of being a baby machine. I'll be hemorrhaging the whole pregnancy, while this guy never comes home. I've done my stint for Dan."

It was 1973. Abortion was quick, easy, legal and inexpensive. She didn't need Dan's permission, and for the first time in their married life she didn't ask for it.

• 7 •

Dan was a feather in the firm's cap, practically a celebrity. The trouble was Gray Cary didn't want to pay him anything extra. They said it would demoralize the staff.

He started at seventeen thousand dollars a year, exactly what the other new attorneys were making. It seemed to Betty that they were saying four years of medical school didn't mean a thing.

The baby-sitter wasn't working out either. Since there were two kids, Betty paid her double. By the time she added it up, the sitter was making almost as much as she was, and the kids weren't happy. She quit the job and went back to night work at Black Angus. That way she could give the kids supper herself. It meant working till two or three in the morning, but it was worth it.

At first a high school girl came in around five and stayed till Dan came home. The kids were little and they were asleep early, so he didn't have to do anything for them.

Then Betty met Phyllis Jardel, a red-haired, round-faced lady with kids of her own. Phyllis began minding the kids at night. Betty and Phyllis became friends.

Phyllis noticed that sometimes Betty seemed sad. Once when she came over, Betty had a black eye. It was quite bruised. Betty had a lot of makeup on it. "What happened?" Phyllis asked at first. Betty didn't answer. She didn't really want to talk about it. "Oh, you know, it was an accident," she finally said. "I stumbled or something."

The neighborhood was deteriorating. When someone robbed the Bank of America and had a shoot-out right in front of the apartment-complex swimming pool, Betty decided that it was time to move. She found a small place on a cul-de-sac in Clairmont, a suburb of San Diego. Even though the rent was low and Dan was finally earning some money, they could still hardly afford it because of all the loan repayments. At last they were able to qualify for credit cards, so they could charge some new furniture. Betty redid the front yard and planted a vegetable garden in the back. She even bought a used washer and dryer with the money she had earned at Black Angus. Their dreams were finally beginning to materialize.

It was the first Christmas they had money to buy other people gifts. "I feel like I'm finally saying thank you for all our parents have done for us," Betty said. Every dime she earned was spent on Christmas gifts to send to her family in New York and to Dan's family in Pittsburgh.

One night right before Christmas Dan agreed to go with Betty to choose the last two gifts for his parents. Betty called a neighborhood teenager to stay with the children for an hour.

Kim was already asleep. The baby-sitter was watching Dan's new TV in the living room. She walked into the kitchen to get something to eat. The TV sparked and set the curtains behind it on fire. The baby-sitter grabbed Kim and Lee. They got out just before the windows exploded. The heat alone could have killed them within a few minutes. The whole front of the house was engulfed in flames.

When Betty and Dan got home, they could hardly believe it. Betty's first feeling was panic, sheer, wild terror. Then she saw the children standing in the dark crying. "Thank God they got out safely," she kept saying. After a while she realized that all of the new furniture in the house was ruined and every single Christmas gift was completely destroyed. She felt happy and miserable at the same time. For days she kept crying. Her emotions were in an uproar. Then she discov-

41

ered that once again she was pregnant. This time, especially after what had happened, she was ready for another baby.

As soon as the insurance company heard who Dan was, they couldn't be helpful enough. They agreed to move them somewhere else and pay for everything. They could almost live on Dan's salary. Betty could still keep the job working at Black Angus for a while. With another baby on the way they really would need a bigger place anyhow.

• 8 •

The next step up was La Jolla, Spanish for "the jewel." Ever since the 1920s La Jolla, with its rugged coastline and hills, had been a favorite spot for the rich and famous. Betty loved the art center, the world-famous museum, the high-style boutiques, and the international restaurants.

Life in La Jolla's fast lane looked casual, but was actually very stressful. Even mismatched clothes had to be strictly designer. Joggers wore headphones for financial reports and beepers so that they wouldn't miss a call.

Almost everyone in La Jolla came from somewhere else. No one knew each other, except by what they wore or owned. Shopping was the main recreation. It seemed to fill an empty place at the core of people's lives. A person gained status by the clothes he wore and the house he lived in, no matter how heavily mortgaged it was. It was not unusual for people to spend so much money on their mortgage that they couldn't afford to furnish the house. In La Jolla it was easy for yuppies with credit cards to forget their own parents' blue-collar origins and values.

La Jolla seemed like the realization of all her dreams, a place where the newly rich could join hands with movie stars, politicians, and old money. Thanksgiving was often celebrated on the beach. The men played football in bathing suits and dinner jackets. The women carved the turkey and set out sterling silver on low bridge tables. Whenever they wanted a drink, the men could walk through the walnut doors of the La Jolla Beach and Tennis Club. The place was steeped in tradition, an elegant mixture of nonchalance and emptiness.

When Dan and Betty bought their tract house in La Jolla, the money the insurance company gave them hardly made a dent. They needed a mortgage for the down payment and another mortgage to finance the house. They were still getting credit card bills every month for the ruined furniture. The mortgage payments were so high, they couldn't keep up with the credit card debt. New furniture was out. They couldn't even afford to heat the place. All that winter everybody walked around wearing hats and coats and gloves. When Dan's brother, Larry, visited, he bought them a set of patio furniture. They used it outside during the day, then carried it into the living room to sit on every night. Betty didn't care. She loved the place. They finally had a real home in a great neighborhood.

Dan was also proud of the house, a two-story with a three-car garage, four bedrooms, and a bonus playroom upstairs. It was a big place, about three thousand square feet with a large yard. It didn't matter that all the houses in the tract were mirror images of each other. After seven years the good life had arrived.

She built a sandbox with her own hands and spent the money she earned baby-sitting on a fancy wooden swing set. She named the new baby, their first son, Daniel T. Broderick IV. Betty tried working at the steakhouse as a hostess again, but she had varicose veins from all the pregnancies and couldn't take the standing.

Finally she went on disability and just stayed home. When Danny was just a few months old, she began doing day care for another little boy his age. Then another. After all, she told Dan, "My degree was in early childhood education. I love taking care of kids, and now I have a beautiful place to do it in."

Before long she had started her own informal day-care center. Most of the mothers didn't really work. They were neighborhood women. Her house was very popular with the kids. She called her little operation Time Out. Mothers could go to lunch, play tennis, just do stuff and have somewhere to leave the children. She charged a dollar an hour and tried to limit it to six or seven kids a day. It was hard to say no. Sometimes she ended up with eleven or twelve little ones at a time besides her own. It was a real fun place for kids to be. The women became Betty's friends, and the children became Danny's.

• 9 •

Dan was always busy with lunches, parties, tennis games, and bars. He was acting more and more like a stranger. Almost never home. "During all the years of our marriage," Betty said finally, "I gave you time. I kept the house clean. I kept the kids quiet. I always made excuses for you. I believed that our life would change once you were a lawyer, but you're more distant now than ever."

"It's all mandatory. That's how it goes," he said coldly.

Betty looked at him. It wasn't that she didn't believe him. She knew he had to do a lot of these things, but she couldn't get past a feeling that there was something else.

"Dan," she said. "When are you here? Not days, not nights, not weekends. I thought by this time we'd really have a marriage. When my father worked and earned money, he was doing it for us, to clothe us and entertain us and take care of us. That was his pride and joy. You want me to believe the same thing about you, but the truth is that you're doing it for yourself, not for the family. You think you can ignore us year after year and as long as you pay the bills I have nothing to complain about. But I'm lonely, Dan. I miss my family in New York. I feel too isolated here. I want to move back there. If you won't come, I'll take the kids and go without you."

It was a strong statement, and it made Dan nervous. To please Betty he agreed to go to a marriage encounter weekend. Someone from the church took care of the kids. Betty was amazed that he said yes. Dan hated church functions. Church turned him off so much that he hadn't wanted a Catholic wedding. He hadn't wanted the children christened. He was even resentful that Betty had First Communion with the girls.

This time Dan said, "I'll try because I don't want to lose what we have."

"I don't want to either," Betty whispered. "I just want more time to love you. I want the kids to have more time to love you. I want my husband, that's all I want."

The weekend was an intense experience. They spent more time together than they had in years. There were group encounter sessions, then each person went to a separate room and wrote letters to the other, expressing their deepest feelings and needs. Betty wrote,

Dearest Dan:

Do you remember how touched and thrilled I was with the gold chain that says, 'I love you more than yesterday, less than tomorrow'? That chain is probably my most treasured possession. I cling to it, hoping it's still true or will come again. . . . You are unique in the world. The first moment I saw you, I loved you; spoke to you, it stayed; wrote to you, it grew; dated you, it got only better and better. No one else I ever met before or since was as right as you. . . .

I love you and want to share all that I am with you. I also need to be loved by you and feel that I know everything there is to know about you, like no one else on earth ever has or ever will. Every day I live with you I want to get a little closer to that goal. The number-one thing I loved about you was how much you loved me and showed it. You know all the rest. . . . I love everything about you now as I did then, except that you don't show your love for me. . . .

45

From his own room, unaware of what Betty was writing, Dan wrote,

> Dear Betts:
> I firmly believe that given time I will become a good husband, father, etc. I tell myself I've got to earn a decent living, establish myself as a lawyer, accrue certain necessary possessions before I can indulge in the luxury of being an attentive, thoughtful person. . . .

Dan said he believed that money would make their lives together happier. They could travel to Europe together and take the whole family to South Bend each year for the Notre Dame game. They could buy whatever they wanted.

The problem, Dan said, was that he might not make it soon enough. He'd been feeling lately that death was approaching. More than anything, Dan added, he wanted to live long enough to pay Betty back for all of the sacrifices she had made.

> To die now would be a tragedy. . . . I want to be the kind of person who will genuinely be missed when he dies. . . . I know that I'm not that person yet. I believe, perhaps foolishly, that I will be someday, but I need time.

They exchanged letters and talked about their feelings. Then they headed home with instructions from the counselors to spend ten minutes a day talking or just holding hands and being close.

"I'm sorry," he told her a few days later, "I'd really like to spend ten minutes a day with you, Betts. You'd be the first person that I'd spend it with. But I just really don't have the time."

Betty needed nurturing and she wasn't getting it. For the first time people who knew them noticed she was becoming critical of Dan in public. Small stuff. Just taking him down a peg, correcting his grammar, making fun of his early Pennsylvania training, that kind of thing.

He was still her only intimate friend on earth, her best friend. She was proud of him and angry at him at the same time. Behavior that once seemed acceptable no longer did.

The low point came one day when she was taking care of half a dozen kids and started hemorrhaging.

"Dan," she said apologetically, calling him at work, "I'm sorry to bother you, but it's an emergency. I think I'm having a miscarriage and I've got six kids here. Can you come home and help me?"

Reluctantly Dan came. Just by chance Vicky Curry, one of the mothers, also arrived. He was annoyed. He saw Vicky and thought Betty didn't really need him. The blood was all over her clothes, her legs, her shoes, and the grass. She was afraid to come into the house because she didn't want to mess up the rug. Betty leaned on the back door for support.

"Dan," she whispered, "the doctor said I should get right over the hospital, but I can hardly walk."

"You can still drive, can't you?" he said, looking up from his *Time* magazine.

"Drive?" she said incredulously. "I'm about to pass out.

He looked down and saw the blood at her feet. "Okay," he said. "I'll get a towel to protect the car seat and I'll take you."

• 10 •

Dan was on a fast track. It wouldn't be long before they'd offer him a partnership. If he accepted, he'd never leave. He wanted to get out, but he was afraid to make the change.

"Look," Betty said. "It's a good firm, the best in town, but you can go faster and farther alone. Whatever you want you can do. That's your magic."

"I want to leave," he told her. "I want to go out on my own and make millions."

"Then I'll help you. We'll do it together," she said. The thought of helping him made her happy. She was starting to feel close to him, reliving the old dreams again.

They'd be risking everything, but they had taken risks before and come out winners. It meant giving up the regular paycheck, the only one they could count on. Betty knew the mortgage payments and bills would still have to be paid each month. There would be start-up costs for an office—rent, overhead, furniture. They'd be back to taking loans, they might lose the house. She'd hate to have that happen, but she loved the challenge. She especially loved having a place in Dan's life again.

"When you were at Gray Cary," she said, "you were working twice as many hours as anyone else, and you were locked into their pay scale. It was crazy. I agreed to the whole medical-law-school thing so we could be way ahead of the other lawyers, not stuck in their system."

"You know, you have beautiful eyes," Dan said. He walked toward her and kissed her. She felt the old flood of feeling. He could still do that to her, bring her to her knees in a heartbeat.

"You'll knock 'em dead," Betty whispered passionately.

He was her key to success. It was almost like rediscovering her own ambition. She was fiercer than he ever imagined. Fiercer right now than he was.

"It won't take long to get the ball rolling," Betty told him. "You're a hot-shot M.D., J.D. Everyone knows you. All your clients will follow you."

Betty chose the office in a big new building, the best and most expensive in town. The rent was more than their mortgage. "They already have a shared secretarial service in the building," she said. "You'll need a phone, business cards, stationery, and you'll need furniture."

The next week Dan went out and chose some light-wood office furniture with metal legs. Betty had other ideas. "Leave it to me," she told him. "You'll start your solo career at the top." She took a crash course in decorating and got her decorator's license, which entitled her to a discount, then she took Dan to L.A. to shop.

Betty picked out the most expensive furniture they had, a magnificent dark-oak parquet desk with a rolltop console behind it, and a wall unit with file drawers in the bottom. She chose brass and pewter bric-a-brac, silk-flower arrangements, and two side chairs covered with Scotch plaid. To that she added several expensive side tables and chairs. Next she ordered blue carpeting and burlap over dark-green glossy wallpaper. The place was handsome, much nicer than what they had at home. It looked like money. It even smelled expensive. Betty wanted an opening party. Dan wouldn't hear of it.

"I don't want anybody eating or drinking in there. They might mess it up. We can't afford what we've got, let alone having to replace anything. We're still poor."

"I know that," she said, laughing. "But your clients won't know it."

She was right. The image of success bred success. Almost immediately the name Daniel Broderick IV, Esquire, became a synonym in San Diego for status. Dan was the hot new malpractice lawyer. People who would never have thought of filing a claim were doing it just to have their name linked with his. He made more money in the first three months on his own than he had made at Gray Cary, Ames and Frye in a year.

Betty was thrilled. No one had handed it to them. It was a life they had built. The two of them had worked together for fourteen years. Now Dan was the man everyone was after, and she was the woman behind him. Betty knew she had made it happen.

Business was booming. The money was pouring in. They were euphoric, celebrating, literally celebrating. Betty bought expensive clothes and earrings, a fur jacket, and had a luncheon for her girlfriends in the backyard. They took weekend trips to San Francisco.

Jimmy Millikin, an attorney, referred a case to Dan that contributed a good deal with very little work. To say thank you, they were supposed to take the Millikins skiing for a weekend. Somehow the ski weekend was transformed to a trip to Europe for three weeks, first-class airfare, five-star hotels, meals, all on Dan.

He was very quiet on that trip. For a guy who had it all, he didn't seem very happy. The self-imposed pressure was building up.

"It must be the pressure," Betty thought. Otherwise it made no sense.

Again he was never home. Again she was gaining weight and nauseated.

"Talk about being caged. You're trapping me just like your father trapped your mother," Betty said when Dan finally walked in drunk at two A.M. "It's the old barefoot-and-pregnant routine. I just can't be what your mother was, money or not. I'm not doing this. Before I married you, I wanted ten kids. But I thought I'd have a husband, a father for my ten kids. I wanted one big happy family with a father like my father. A father who played basketball and took us to the beach and took us out on Sundays and did everything with my mother as a family." Dan didn't answer. He just stared at her.

"You've never changed a baby yet. You've never fed a baby, you don't even like them. You don't like the toys, you don't like the mess, you don't like the noise. Your father didn't like them either. But he liked the idea that there was a Christmas card every year with all those names on it that proved what a man he was because he had turned out all those babies. Not me," Betty said. "We have three children. I'm not spending my whole marriage throwing up in the toilet." Suddenly she was crying. "This is my last baby. After this I swear I'll never do it again."

Phlebitis set in, another difficult pregnancy. On top of that she needed a C-section. Betty kept her word. This time, after little Rhett was born, she had her tubes tied.

She had just gotten home, still had the clamps in her belly, the night Dan and his friend took the kids out for pizza. It got later and later. She thought they'd be back in an hour. Suddenly it was raining like mad and almost midnight. She kept thinking of Dan drunk in a bar with her kids. Danny wasn't even three yet. She imagined him driving home drunk on the wet roads with the kids tired and crying in the backseat. Maybe it was hormones or having four children or postpartum blues or having her tubes tied or an-

50

other baby to tie her down. All she knew was she kept getting mad-der and madder.

"You son of a bitch," she yelled when he finally came in. "You're going to kill my kids." She picked up the stereo turntable and threw it across the room.

• 12 •

Dan was making more money than ever. The progression was so rapid, it made Betty's head spin. She decorated the kitchen with fancy brick flooring, dark-wood cabinets, white ceramic knobs, and im-ported, hand-painted-tile counters. She worked very hard at it and was very proud. They also added a swimming pool. They had money for maids, they owned five cars, they traveled to Europe, Bermuda, and Cancún. They joined the best country clubs, they bought a boat and a ski condo. Now they not only attended charity affairs but they hosted full tables and invited all their friends.

Dan joined the board of directors of the bar association. He wrote a regular column for them. He had become "the authority" on personal injury and malpractice and one of the richest lawyers in San Diego. He had really done it. He was earning a million dollars a year and he wasn't forty. He had no distractions and no pleasures. His family didn't distract him. His friends didn't distract him. Sports didn't distract him. He was a racehorse with blinders. Now that he had achieved it, Dan suddenly found that he had no other goals in his life. He was at the top of the mountain. There was nowhere else to go. He always thought that when he got there and made his million dollars a year, he would be happy. All of a sudden he no longer had a purpose. Now he could do anything and he still wasn't happy.

On a whim in an airport in Denver Dan bought himself a Diesel-dorf. It looked exactly like a 1930 Mercedes. He saw it on display with ropes around it and thought it matched his image. Then he started looking at Rolls-Royces.

Betty still liked her Ford Suburban. She used it to take the kids dirt-biking. She could get five dirt bikes in the back. The license plate said LODEMUP, and that's exactly what she did.

She'd graduated from sports cars. She was maturing. Her life was what it was supposed to be, a continuum. Betty was coming into her own as a woman. She had money and now she had freedom, because after nine pregnancies she finally wasn't pregnant every year.

Dan seemed mad at her for having such a good time in life. Her youngest child was four. She was feeling good about herself and everyone else. Dan seemed to hate losing that control over her. As long as they were broke and she was pregnant, her options in life were very limited. Now she was getting involved in activities on her own. She was starting to meet people.

She thought Dan was afraid that she'd become too successful and have power and money of her own. He seemed very threatened by that prospect. Extremely threatened. She was at a jumping-off point, about to get on with the next stage of her life. It was time to do something worthwhile for herself while she could still look like a million bucks. Betty had an idea—she'd start a children's store. She'd call it Cherubs. She even had the site and the sign picked out. She was going to Europe to buy baby clothes for the grandmothers in La Jolla. Dan was furious. Betty thought it was because if she went out and started doing things, she'd have choices. That, she decided, scared him, because he knew how difficult he was.

• 13 •

In a few more years, Betty liked to say, the girls would be summering in Europe, skiing in Vale, and going to fine colleges. She and Dan

52

would be flying back and forth to football games and parents' week-ends. The kids would come home with their fiancés, and then they'd do the family wedding. After that they would become grandparents, just as her parents and Dan's parents had. Actually Lee was only eleven and Kim was thirteen, but Betty liked looking forward to the future.

Dan didn't see it that way. He didn't have a long-term picture of his life from cradle to grave. Now that he had money, he wanted to go back and live his youth over again. He wanted to be free and rich and young. He was drunk every night. Dan was happiest when he was drunk. He had so much inner tension. This seemed to be his main release. When he wasn't drunk, he was crazed, screaming, and break-ing things. That's why she had put up with his drinking for so long. But somehow lately Betty was getting more and more fed up with his drunkenness and his never coming home.

Friday nights were the worst. A mandatory drunk, she called it. He didn't care whom he was with, where he was, or what he drank. If it was Friday night, Dan Broderick was drunk.

Betty thought they had a responsibility to these children to act more mature. "How can I raise our children not to drink and drive," she said, "when their father's up on the sidewalk, going up and down streets the wrong way and backing into trees?"

"You used to think it was cute when I got drunk," he said, stagger-ing toward her.

"Yes, because when you were drunk, you'd be slobbering all over my neck and telling me you wanted to sleep with me. But as the years went on, I got disgusted. You don't even know who I am. Let's do it sober. Let's know who we are for a change."

Betty was no longer interested in sex, because Dan was always drunk. She even locked him out once. He was so drunk that night, he hardly knew what was happening, just passed out in the car in the garage. She was putting her foot down, finally taking a stand about drinking.

PART III

•••

The Affair

"Nineteen eighty-three is when Dan's affair started. Everything fell apart, and it never let up. I've done almost ten years on this case and the hardest time I served was before the crimes."

—*Betty Broderick after she was convicted and sentenced*

• 1 •

"Wow," Dan said, whistling softly under his breath, "Isn't she beautiful?" He was talking to the guy standing next to him at a cocktail
party. Betty turned to look. All she could see was the back of a tall,
thin girl, long blond hair, and a strange new flushed look on Dan's
face.

He's probably just had too much to drink again, she thought. Betty had
a lot of gorgeous friends, even a former Miss America, who was so
beautiful, she got out of the shower looking great, and she'd never
heard Dan comment on any of them. She walked to the other side of
the room to get a better look. *God,* she thought. *That girl looks like I
used to look at nineteen or twenty.* She stood there for a minute taking
in the high cheekbones; the long, straight nose; green eyes; and the
gorgeous smile that exposed perfect white teeth and soft pink gums.

"Who's that?" she asked, raising her eyebrows and gesturing toward the girl.

"Just a kid," he answered, then his eyes glazed over. "An innocent
cherub who answers the phones down in the lobby at the office. Too
bad she can't type. I'd hire her in a minute."

"Oh, the office girl," Betty said haughtily. Dan's response had set
off an alarm inside her head. She tried to let it pass. Her reaction
might have been stronger if she wasn't so busy getting ready for a trip
with the kids. They'd been planning it all year. Most of it had been
mapped out on paper months before. They were scheduled to leave
as soon as school got out. There was still so much to do that Betty
didn't really think about the girl again till the morning of the trip.

There was something strange about the way Dan took her face in
his hands and said good-bye. Something final about it, a momentary
sadness or regret, almost a tenderness. She could feel it in the way his
lips touched hers. Then it was gone. He was tense and in a hurry to

57

see them off. Betty let that pass too. She had songs, games, maps, tour books. Even Erma Bombeck and Joyce Maynard, just in case there was any time for herself.

All four kids were talking at once as she glanced in the rearview mirror and saw Dan walking quickly back into the house. Then, for a minute Betty thought of the girl and wished she wasn't going to Colorado and Montana, but Dan wasn't a girl chaser. Besides, who could be bothered? It was silly to worry. There were waterfalls, mountains, canyons, glaciers. They would fish and river-raft, climb and pitch tents. She wasn't just sending her kids off to camp. She'd be right there camping with them. It was all part of being the perfect mother. She had even decorated the interior of the Chevy Suburban for the long ride.

"It's a special summer," Betty said to Dan the night before. "It's an ideal time for me and the kids to do this. The kids' ages work better now than they ever will again. Rhett's not a baby anymore, and Kim's not quite a full-blown teenager. By next year Kim would probably rather be doing something else. The only thing I wish is that you could be with us."

Betty knew that Dan had no interest in being away for five weeks even if he had the time. At least he'd scheduled two weekend trips. He'd fly out and meet them first in Keystone, Colorado, then in Flathead, Montana. Anticipation of those weekends and her love of the kids and adventure would sustain her.

At first they had a great time. They stopped at Cousin Joe's in Tempe, Arizona, and spent the night. The kids made cupcakes. In between the fun of camping there was a lot of hard work pitching tents, doing laundry, preparing food, and breaking up fights. Still, there was a huge gap in her life. She was waiting for Colorado and Montana, waiting for Dan. During the first visit in Colorado Dan acted funny. Again she brushed it off.

"You're grumpy," she said gently. "I'll rub your back. I think you're tired. This weekend is just too short."

When she saw him in Montana, things were worse. Instead of just being distant, Dan was hostile. He criticized everything she did, seemed annoyed that she was even breathing.

"You're acting like a real jerk," Betty finally said. "I've been waiting for you, missing you, wanting to talk to you and sleep with you. Stop tearing me apart. I was doing fine when you weren't here. If you're going to be here, then be here." After that there was a lot of silence between them. The things she'd been bursting to tell him just went unsaid. All Dan seemed to want was to escape.

He's been moody and tired before, Betty told herself. *No tragedy. It's not the end of the world.* She went right back to thinking all the problems would go away if she just kept a happy, positive attitude.

There was trouble during the last part of the trip. About one hundred miles past Las Vegas the car started smoking and overheating. She tried putting in water; it didn't help, just kept leaking out. They were in the desert, and it was over one hundred degrees Fahrenheit. The kids were hot and tired. Betty was hot and tired. Camping, tents, restaurants, motels, waterfalls, canyons—everything seemed old now. She was almost out of money and dying to see Dan. The local gas station said it would cost seven hundred dollars to fix the car. Not even a year old, it had thirteen thousand miles on it. *It might be covered under the warranty,* Betty thought. *I'd better call Dan.*

No answer. Betty took the kids back to the motel and kept calling. Day and night. Still no answer. The motelkeeper offered to help. "The guy at the gas station is a crook," he said. "Don't let him do the work. He'll just be stealing your money." They ended up being towed to another gas station in Las Vegas. The whole family in the car riding backward for over 100 miles. Big help. She felt like an idiot.

They finally had the work done. Betty tried to keep the kids busy. She kept calling the house. She also tried to stay calm. Where the hell was he? Why was it taking two days to fix the car? She had to get home. On top of the strange, panicky feeling about Dan, they had an important wedding to go to in Newport Beach.

Betty pulled into the driveway at eleven-thirty, the night before the wedding. She knew Dan heard them. She saw him at the window, but he didn't come out. When Betty got out of the car, she stood in the dark driveway for a minute. Everything was completely still. The kids were all asleep. Instead of joy she felt a dead, dark silence. "I'm in

59

trouble," she said to the night air. Betty could hear her heart beating. She didn't know whether to run to the front door and demand an answer about where Dan had been or throw herself into his arms. She began to tremble. She thought of getting back into the car and leaving again till she figured out how to handle things.

"Hi, darling," she called, opening the door. "We're home." No answer. "I'm really proud of myself. I made it back before the wedding. You'll never guess what happened to the car. Boy, am I glad to be home," she continued without missing a beat. "I've missed you so much. I tried to call a zillion times, but you were never here."

Dan still didn't say a word. Didn't even stand up. "I'm so glad to be home," Betty repeated.

The next morning on the drive to the wedding, he finally looked at her. She smiled, hoping he'd say, "Boy, you look great. I don't know how you do it. You haven't even unpacked the car, you've barely slept, and you're gorgeous. What a dress! What a woman!" For sixteen years she had been hoping for that. Instead he had a tight, pained expression on his face. His eyes narrowed slightly. The corners of his mouth turned down.

"What's the problem, Dan," Betty finally asked. "This is supposed to be an exciting day. We're on the way to celebrate life, love, friendship, marriage."

"Get fucked," he snapped. "Life with you sucks. You're fat, old, boring, ugly, and stupid." Betty's eyes opened wider.

"I'm thirty-five years old and I wear a size eight, so I can't be very fat for someone five foot eleven," she said. "I'm very bubbly, I have a lot of fun with everyone, big people and little people. I prefer little people. Everyone always says I'm pretty, and I know I'm not stupid."

"I'm sick of you. I'm sick of the kids. I'm sick of the house. I wanna throw in the towel."

Betty could feel pressure building up inside her head like steam pushing through pipes that are too narrow.

"Stop it," she wanted to shout. Her eyes filled with tears. She wiped them away. They hardened.

So who's skipping down the street? she thought. *What's wrong with you, you son of a bitch? What the hell have you been doing while I've been*

60

pitching tents with your four kids? But she didn't say any of it. She was afraid of a confrontation, afraid of facing the truth. Betty was still hoping that if she ignored it, maybe it would go away. Her head tilted slightly to the right, and a waxlike smile formed on her lips. After that they were both absolutely silent. It seemed like hours before Dan parked in front of the church.

"Well," she said opening the car door, "we're finally here."

• 2 •

All the next week Dan got into a new thing. He completely avoided her. Maybe it wasn't so new, she thought. Maybe she was just noticing it for the first time. One night he came home drunk.

"I've hired an assistant," he announced. The words were slurred.

"Oh, that's great," she said, jumping up from the coach and hugging him. "I just know things will be better. It will take some of the pressure off. You'll have more time to spend with me and the kids. Wait till I tell them. They're going to be so happy."

It wasn't that he had no help. Sharon Stubbs worked for him part-time. She was a dedicated, terrific secretary, but Dan never wanted to make a commitment by hiring her officially. He kept her employed as an independent contractor. That way he could avoid giving her fringe benefits, such as profit sharing, medical insurance, or parking. The hourly rate was good. She needed the money. So she put up with it. Sharon worked in a little cubicle wearing a headphone and typing her heart out.

"I know you've always been a one-man band, but you really needed a secretary. I'm thrilled. Who is it?"

Dan swayed unsteadily on his feet. "Linda," he answered, "the receptionist."

An image of the gorgeous kid at the cocktail party flashed into her head. Then the shock hit. Instantly she understood it all—why he'd become so distant, why she hadn't been able to reach him for days, why he'd decided to hire someone.

"You don't mean *the* Linda?" she repeated, feeling a surge of panic. "The one from the downstairs lobby who can't even type?"

• 3 •

Betty had her sources. She started checking around. Linda Kolkena came from a Catholic family somewhere in the Midwest. Her father didn't believe in girls going to college. There was an older sister named Margaret out in Oregon and a couple of brothers. Her mother died of cancer at thirty-nine when Linda was still a teenager. That's when she got wild and began running around. Her father remarried. Linda decided her stepmother was a witch. She quit high school and took off. She lied about her age and got a job as a stewardess for Delta Airlines. They fired her when someone found her drunk on a male passenger's lap.

A reliable source, an editor's daughter, told Betty she was walking past the county jail with Linda once when some of the inmates whistled. Linda picked up her skirt, shouted obscene things to them, and laughed. A man who took her to a party said it was a wild night. She got drunk, did drugs, and was generally out of hand.

Linda lived in Pacific Beach in an old wooden house with a man named Charles from Australia and a woman named Eva. Eva's boyfriend, Rick, also lived there. Linda had no money. She rode a bike to work.

More than anything Betty wanted Dan back. She tried harder than ever, walking on eggshells, seeking approval. Dan said "fat," Betty practically stopped eating. Linda had long hair, Betty decided to let her hair grow back to the way it was in college. Dan said "old," she called a plastic surgeon, one of Dan's clients, and asked for help getting rid of the wrinkles that were hardly even there. She got braces to fix her one crooked tooth and began to think about a brow lift and a tummy tuck. She wanted to be nineteen again and perfect, absolutely perfect, for Dan. He became colder, more distant, and more abusive.

Betty began reading books on midlife crises, recognizing Dan on every page. All Dan's friends also seemed to be having affairs and getting divorced.

"I know you're unhappy, Dan," she said, "but please read these books. Let's go to counseling. We've got to straighten this out." When that didn't work, Betty said, "I think it was a huge mistake hiring Linda. It's bad enough you're infatuated with someone in the same building, but now you're paying her all this money just to be near you for twelve or fourteen hours every day with no one else around."

Dan still didn't answer, but he looked uncomfortable. At least it was an opening.

"How would you feel," she continued, "if I overpaid some hunk to work in our house twelve hours a day with just him and me at home alone, undisturbed?" Just saying it out loud made Betty think of Linda parading around while Dan watched and fantasized. Her voice got higher, more strident. She knew he'd feel challenged, but it was too late. It was like watching a movie of herself. She could see what was happening, but she couldn't stop it. "Get rid of her," Betty yelled. "I'll give you three weeks. I want her out of there by October first, or you're out of this house."

"Lady," he shouted back, his eyes like stone, "you're crazy, you're losing it." He began to walk away, then turned toward her again and wrapped his arms across his chest. "Get fucked," he yelled, staring her down like a dog. "It's *my* house. If you don't like things my way, *you* can get out."

Dan was late every night that week. On Friday he announced he was going to Oregon for the weekend. The next day Betty got a call from a friend. "I missed you last night at the black-tie opening party. I sent the invitation to both of you, but Dan showed up with this gorgeous girl, said she was his personal assistant and you were busy. They came and left together. You'd better watch out."

Betty never found out where Dan was the rest of that weekend. Sunday night when he walked in all-smiles, she was shaking again. "What's the matter with you," he asked. She told him. "Give me a break," he moaned, rolling his eyes. "Linda was just going to the same party. I can't control where she goes. She volunteered to drive me to the airport, so we left together. Man, you're really losing it. Your wheels are coming off."

Betty was confused. What she felt and saw and suspected was all one way, but Dan kept denying it. Either he wasn't coming home until very late or he was sneaking out at night.

"You look tired," he said to her one night at about nine o'clock. "Why don't you go to bed?"

"I am tired," she admitted. Three hours later she woke up to go to the bathroom and he was gone.

On her thirty-sixth birthday he didn't come home at all and didn't even call. Betty cooked dinner and served it to the children. She tried to cover up. So did they. They bought her her favorite flowers. They wanted to make her feel better. Danny told her how pretty she looked in her new dress. They took turns with the camera so that she'd have pictures of herself with each one of them. Lee brought out the cake and candles, Rhett told jokes and sang happy birthday. The empty feelings rose in the room like the smoke from the burned-out candles.

Dan has never been this cruel before, Betty thought as she put the kids to bed. Rhett was last. She leaned over and pressed her cheek against his. "My little stand-up comic is finally lying down," she said. He put his arms around her neck. "Happy birthday, Mommy," he whispered, then his eyes filled with tears. "I'm sorry Daddy didn't come home."

There were some old pills in the medicine cabinet. She couldn't remember what they were. Maybe Seconal or Prozac from when the baby died. Betty didn't even look at the labels. It didn't matter. She undid the cap and poured them into the palm of her hand. She took them slowly, deliberately, one at a time, with water in between. She didn't want to screw this up, she didn't want to throw up. Betty wasn't sure what she did want besides Dan and his love. Dan and the children were all that had any meaning to her. After she swallowed the pills, she went into the guest bedroom to lie down. He would come looking for her as soon as he got home.

Strange thoughts began moving around in her head. For a minute she was six again. Her father was scooping her up in his arms, kissing her. Then it was Dan kissing her on their first date. Betty got up and started walking unsteadily toward the bathroom. Her legs felt stiff, mechanical, like a baby learning to walk. She wasn't sure if this was part of a dream or if she was really walking.

There was dull pressure in the back of her head, and she felt dizzy. Betty picked up Dan's razor. She held it at arm's length. She examined it, then came a very strong feeling. She wanted to cut those veins, bleed out the pain, make it all stop. It was hard to concentrate, hard to keep her eyes open and the razor in her hand. She put it against her wrist and pressed down, then hesitated for a minute. Betty winced. She pressed down and moved the edge of the razor. She saw the blood start to spurt out over the white skin of her wrist. It burned. She stopped, startled by the stinging and the blood. She tried again, just below the first cut, and again above it. She moved the razor to her left hand and began to cut the vein on her right wrist. It was hard to hold the razor with her left hand, and it hurt when she began to cut. Betty felt a sudden wave of dizziness.

Oh, God, she thought, *I've got to make it back to the bed. It would scare the kids to find me on the bathroom floor.* She began walking with her wrists up. She didn't want to make a mess. White and black spots were all she could see. Betty reached out and felt for the mattress and pillow. She fell back onto the bed. The pillow felt soft against the back of her head, wonderfully soft. She thought about Rhett with the tears in his eyes. Her baby, her last one, how much she loved him, curled up beside her. She could almost feel Rhett's eyelashes against her cheek. She could almost feel his warm little face next to hers and the air he breathed out as she breathed it in. Then even the images of Rhett started getting blurry. Betty was trying hard to hold on to Rhett, to keep him from fading into blackness, but she couldn't.

"Holy shit, Betts, what the hell have you done?" Dan's voice sounded far away. He was shaking her. The room was light. She tried to open her eyes. She closed them again. Her lids felt heavy. Her head ached. The bed was full of dried blood. She raised her hands and saw that it had dripped down her arms all the way to the elbows. When Dan saw the blood, there were tears in his eyes. "I'm sorry," he said. "I wish you hadn't done that. What the hell would the kids do without you?"

His head was on her shoulder. She felt his tears on her neck. "I love you, darling, don't cry," she whispered. Now she was comforting him. She kissed him. It was a warm, soft kiss full of sadness. For the first time she thought he was really scared. He must still love her. He must. After all, he was crying.

"I've missed you so much," she sobbed. Then Dan moved away. He looked at her. "Betts," he said slowly, deliberately. "You're very sick. You've been imagining things about me and Linda. She's just a sweet, innocent girl. I hired her because she got fired from her other job answering the phones and I felt sorry for her. She's very intelligent and a great help to me, but there's nothing going on. You really need help. You're having a breakdown."

More than anything Betty wanted to believe Dan. Compared with Linda, a breakdown would be welcome. She listened to him, still dazed, her eyes fixed on his. She took his hand and tried to hold on to it. Her left wrist ached. He saw her wince. "Come, let's wash this off and get it bandaged," he said. She sat up. "God, I've made a mess here," she said. The old hangdog, foolish-little-girl feeling was back again. Like a child in the presence of someone very wise and old. She promised Dan she'd call a doctor that afternoon and arrange to get some help. As soon as he left for work, she called a therapist. Dan was too busy to go with her, so she went alone.

"Dr. Breckenridge, I'm a nervous wreck," she said. "Just trying to talk about it has me shaking all over again. I know I'm not coping very well. I don't know where I stand anymore. I know by my intuition and by all these obvious clues that Dan is having an affair with this girl, but he keeps denying it. Until now I've never doubted anything Dan ever told me, not ever. If he told me we were rich, I believed it. If he told me we were poor, I believed it. If he told me he had depositions in Oregon for the weekend, I never questioned him. I never called hotels to check up on him. I believed him. I believed everything he ever told me. But now he's telling me black is green and I don't know what to believe. I thought if I confronted him and it was the truth, we could have it out, and it would come to some conclusion, but that's not happening. Dan says I'm going crazy. Dan says my wheels are coming off, I'm having a breakdown."

The doctor nodded. "I understand, Mrs. Broderick. I hear you. But instead of telling me what Dan says, I want you to tell me what you think and feel."

"I don't even know what I feel anymore," Betty answered. "Dan says the problem is not Linda Kolkena, the problem is me. I know I'm older, I'm not nineteen or twenty like she is. So I say, okay, he wants nineteen with long blond hair and no children and no responsibilities. I'll do what I can. I grow my hair, but I can't be nineteen, I can't put the kids back."

"How does that make you feel?" the doctor asked.

"Very depressed, very, very depressed. Dan's opinion of me is all I ever cared about. Before this I thought people liked me. I thought I was pretty. I thought I was reasonably intelligent. I mean, I was not an embarrassment to him. I know the kids like me. In my estimation we have a lovely home, I am a good cook, I'm a good entertainer. I try to be a credit to him the way I expect him to be a credit to me. I'm very proud of him. I want him to be proud of me. He says I'm not pleasing to him anymore. You know, if the problem is that I'm not a good cook, I'll take cooking lessons. If I'm not a good housekeeper,

I'll keep house better. But if he says I'm fat, ugly, stupid, old and boring, then what do I do? All these people keep calling me and telling me they see him with Linda. He keeps saying I'm crazy."

"Betty," the therapist said firmly near the end of the session, "I don't think you're crazy. Get a lawyer. You have got to get a lawyer to protect yourself." If she had taken that advice, her life would probably have turned out very differently. Instead Betty's mouth dropped. "But I don't want a lawyer," she said. "I don't want a divorce. I want Dan. I want my husband. I love him. I want him to get over the girlfriend, go to therapy, get over the mid-life crisis, and come back to us. Why would I hire a lawyer? You only hire a lawyer to file for divorce. I want to fix it." After that Betty stopped therapy.

When Dan came home that night, she brought him a drink. "Honey," she said. "Do you want more children? I've got these problems with my legs, and the pregnancies are tough for me. But, heck, if you want me to have more babies like your mother had. Let's do it. I called the gynecologist, Benito Villanueva, this afternoon. He said the tubal ligation can probably be reversed."

Dan raised his eyes from his glass and looked at her. "God, you really are crazy," he said. "I don't want more kids, shit. I don't even want the ones we've got."

The next day it started all over again. Two more phone calls from friends who were seeing Dan and Linda at lunch together at the best restaurants in town. Betty picked up the phone and called Vicky. "You helped me through the miscarriage," she said, "and I need you again. Dan's having an affair with his office girl. Maybe it's my fault. Maybe I've been too busy with the kids. Maybe I've taken him for granted. After work I know it's customary for a lot of people to meet for a drink or two, and I'm always too busy to go. There are braces this way and piano lessons that way, soccer is in another place. I'm in a sweat suit running all over. I don't have time to get dressed up and meet Dan. Linda Kolkena is available for these things on an everyday basis. He's paying her for the privilege of being in her company twelve, fourteen hours a day. Sometimes he doesn't come home at all."

"Start going down there," Vicky said. "Put on your makeup and your good dresses. Let her know you exist. Don't interfere with his work. Just say, 'Hi, I'm Betty, I'm Dan's wife. I'm alive, it's me.' Go, I'll mind your kids."

"Dan's birthday is November twenty-seventh," Betty answered. "I'll put on a real pretty dress and go down there and surprise him."

• 5 •

"I want a home-cooked roast-beef dinner with a chocolate birthday cake," he told her the night before. Betty did that all morning. She set the table, then she got all fixed up and went down to the office carrying a silver ice bucket, the best bottle of *brut* she could find, and two glasses. She figured Linda would be in the same cubicle that Sharon Stubbs used to use. Betty heard that Sharon had quit when Linda was hired, even though Dan wanted to keep her on for the typing.

She wouldn't talk to Linda at all. That would be demeaning. She'd just walk right past her into Dan's office. That way she'd accomplish two things. She'd make her presence felt and she'd have a few quiet minutes with Dan before he came home and walked into the hive of kids. Betty had never done anything like this before. She thought it would be nice. She even decided to bring the telescope she had bought him for his birthday. He could try it out right there on the view from his office window. She walked past Sharon Stubbs's old cubicle. It was empty. That was the first surprise. Where the desk had been, there was now a refrigerator with a lot of wine and wineglasses, Betty's crystal wineglasses from her wedding. Her stomach tightened. *No Linda, no desk,* she thought.

"Hi," she said to the new receptionist. "I'm Betty, Dan Broderick's wife." She could hear the high, tense edge in her own voice. The receptionist lifted her eyes and took Betty in.

69

"They went out to lunch at eleven," she said. "They're not back yet."

"Who?" Betty asked.

"Just them," the receptionist answered. "Dan and Linda."

"Thank you," Betty said, swaying slightly, holding the silver ice bucket like a life-support cushion. "I'll just wait in his office." As soon as Betty turned around, she saw the name Linda Kolkena in big brass letters on the door of the office right next to Dan's. She looked in. It was a large, very expensive space with the same view as Dan's. There was opulent new furniture and a new stereo system. Now she understood why Sharon quit. She was over there typing her heart out in a little cubicle with no benefits. She couldn't stand the inequity.

On the wall behind the desk Betty saw a large framed picture of Dan taken in 1967 before they were married. He was riding a white horse. The horse was bucking, very macho. The only thing missing was the armor. By the time she got into Dan's office, she had a splitting headache. Streamers and balloons were taped to his desk. There was an open bottle of champagne. A chocolate-mousse cake had been left unfinished. The dirty dishes and glasses were still there. Betty walked back to the receptionist.

"Who was at the party?" she asked.

"No one," the girl answered again. "Just them."

Betty could feel heat surging up into her face. "Thank you," she managed. She walked across the lobby again and back into Dan's office. She closed the door and sat down alone at his desk.

"Oh, God," Betty said softly, "please help me get through this." She was so numb, she didn't know how long she sat there. The sun went down. Dan never came back. No one came, not even a maid to clean up the mess. Finally Betty picked up Dan's phone and dialed Vicky.

"It's worse than I thought," she said.

"What are you going to do?" Vicki asked.

"I have absolutely no idea," Betty answered. "I just don't know."

It wasn't a terrifying sensation. Just a strong, propelling feeling, a strange new force inside her. When she walked into the house, it happened. She went upstairs, straight into the bedroom, and started grabbing Dan's clothes. *I know what I'll do. I'll kick the son of a bitch out.* Dan's closet was on one side of the room. It ran the whole length with mirrors for the doors. It was supposed to be her closet too. But ninety-seven percent of it was filled with his stuff. Her clothes were all scrunched up at the far end. The sliding glass doors to the balcony were on the other side of the room.

"I'll help him pack." Betty said. She began grabbing Dan's clothes by the armload and throwing them over the balcony into the back-yard. First the hand-stitched, hand-monogrammed shirts, then the custom-made suits, sports jackets, and trousers. Then all the fancy matching ski outfits. Lee stood perfectly still in the doorway, her soft brown eyes full of fear. Kim ran over to Betty and grabbed her arms. "Mom, Mom, what are you doing? Stop it, stop, Dad's gonna kill you."

Betty's face was bright red and furious. The tears were streaming down her cheeks. She raised her arms and began flailing them to fend Kim off. "Get out of here, just get out of here," she cried. Kim saw a look in her mother's eyes that frightened her. It made her back away. All the kids knew how important Dan's clothes were to him. They knew he spent hours getting dressed every morning, showering, tweezing his eyebrows, powdering himself. No one was allowed into the room. He always topped it off with a fresh flower in his lapel from the yard that matched the color of his tie. When they went skiing, he carried more stuff than the rest of the family put together. Had to have a different color-coordinated outfit for each day on the slopes. Even carried a small mirror and held it up to make sure he looked okay if he got windblown. Clothes were everything to him.

After the closet was empty, Betty took the drawers with his under-wear and socks and pajamas and dumped them out on top. It was a huge pile. The only things she left in the closet were the top hat and the red, silk-lined cape. She especially wanted to destroy them because Dan loved them so much, but she couldn't do it.

"Fuck Rhett Butler. My next husband's going to be a prince in Saudi Arabia," she yelled as she ran to the garage. She took the can of gasoline for the lawnmower and poured it on the pile. Then Betty struck a match and threw it. Kim and Lee ran away, terrified. Betty stood there, watching the smoke and the flames and crying as if she'd never stop. When the fire finally died down, she took a can of black paint, pried open the top with a screwdriver, and poured it on top of the smoldering ashes.

Dan came home sometime after eight, blind drunk, wobbly-legged, and very happy. He found the front door locked and staggered around to the back like a dog looking for his roast-beef dinner. Betty met him at the door. She was calm now, too calm. "You once told me that all you needed was your red Corvette and your checkbook. Well, you have your Corvette, here's your checkbook. I waited all afternoon at your office. I hope you had fun fucking Linda. I'll be seeing you."

Dan was in shock. He had no idea she'd been down to the office. First he looked confused, then frightened. He sobered up and began to make excuses.

"Jesus Christ," he said."I don't believe you thought that. I don't fucking believe it. We went to lunch together, but then I went to a deposition. I don't even know where Linda went. She must have gone shopping. I swear there's nothing going on." He looked at the pile of burned clothes and acted like they didn't matter. He even went out and brought in a few pieces that weren't burned or ruined, but he didn't get mad. *That's very strange,* Betty thought. *Normally he'd kill me.* Dan just came into the house and kept swearing up and down that there was nothing going on with Linda and that there never had been anything going on.

"You've got to believe me. I'm not even attracted to that kid. I'm old enough to be her father. Come on, Betty, you fuck as good as you fight. There are no other women. It's just you I love. I never even held her hand, I never had a fantasy about her." Dan kissed her and stroked her hair. He put his hand on the small of her back and pulled her tight against him. She began feeling confused, close to him again. She closed her eyes. He kissed her.

In all the years since he'd first kissed her when she was only seventeen, he'd never chased women. He never even seemed interested. *Maybe I am losing it,* she thought.

When the kids came home again, Dan took them into another room and spoke softly to them. He reassured them that everything was okay. He said there would be no divorce and that they didn't have to decide whom they were going to live with. The kids said they couldn't understand why Mommy was being so mean when Daddy had done absolutely nothing wrong. After a few minutes they all came out of the room. Betty served the roast-beef dinner and the chocolate cake. They sang "Happy Birthday" to Dan and sat on the couch for a while. Betty said she'd call the tailor and order all new clothes for him in the morning. Then they went to bed and made love like nothing had ever happened.

• 7 •

Maria, the cleaning woman, and Betty had always understood each other. Betty had also taken Maria's daughter in as if she were her own child and given Maria a home. She had fed her, clothed her, taken her daughter to school. In exchange Maria loved Betty as fiercely as if they were sisters.

When Maria came to work and saw the pile of burned clothing, right away she thought about the girl. The one who came to the house when the Mrs. was away traveling with the children. The one who left her towel and her bathing suit on the chair next to the swimming pool. It was not a question a maid could ask, even if she spoke the same language as the lady of the house, and Maria Montez spoke only Spanish.

Maria cleaned up the mess and waited quietly till Betty Broderick came downstairs.

"*Buenos días,*" Maria said.

"*Buenos días,*" Betty answered.

Yes, Maria thought, *she knows.* Betty was smiling, but her eyes were sad, smoldering like the pile of hot black ashes.

The bravest people are the ones who can overcome fear, Betty told herself. Dan called for a truce between them. Nobody was supposed to mention Linda's name. She worked for him. She had an office. She had benefits. They went to lunch together, and that was all.

Maybe he's getting over it, Betty thought. *Maybe it never happened.* Dan wasn't staying out overnight anymore. He wasn't talking divorce. They were still sleeping together three or four times a week. That hadn't changed. He wasn't even complaining that she was fat, ugly, old, stupid, and boring anymore. Dan's dissatisfaction had found a new focus.

He wanted a bigger house. He didn't want Betty entertaining at the Coral Reef house anymore. He was ashamed they were still living there. He wanted a mansion, not a tract house. Dan suspended the annual Christmas party and the usual dinner parties that they always had. Dan said everything was on hold until they found that magnificent home they were looking for.

Betty loved to give these parties. They were so successful that they were famous. She worked on every detail. The flowers, the china, the cooking—she did it all herself. She impressed these people in San Diego because she knew how to do things that they'd never even heard of. Dan reaped the benefits of all that. All those business people thought he was wonderful to have such fabulous parties and do everything so perfectly while other people had backyard barbecues in T-shirts.

"Why can't we continue doing it?" she asked. "Nobody cares if we don't have a mansion."

"Because I don't feel like it," he answered.

Dan had never said, "This is a really nice party," or "Thank you for inviting my friends," or "You did a good job." In fact a couple of times, just like his father, he'd wait until all the guests were seated and then say something insulting about the dinner. It took all that Betty had not to burst into tears as his mother did when Dan's father had done that to her.

Spring came. Still, nothing pleased him. Betty didn't dare plan a summer trip. She just kept looking for houses. She was trying to be low-key and not get him riled. "I want a mansion with a real crystal chandelier," he kept saying, but he didn't want to pay the price. He bought two lots in Fairbanks Ranch and joined the country club without telling her. Then he announced that that was where he'd build his dream house. "That way, we'll get a three-million-dollar house for five hundred thousand," he said.

"You're wrong," she told him. "Besides, I don't want to move to Fairbanks Ranch. It's all hype." They handed out brochures that talked about exclusivity and security. They showed a lady riding a magnificent horse in full habit in a field of daisies. "But nothing in Fairbanks Ranch looks like that. It's just dirt," Betty said. For years there'll be heavy construction, no schools, no markets, and no easy access to the things we need."

Still, Betty really wanted to settle the house issue, even if it meant moving to Fairbanks Ranch. She missed having the annual Christmas party. She missed entertaining. Underneath she was scared. Maybe it wasn't the house at all. Maybe the house was just an excuse. Maybe it really had something to do with Linda.

Every time she thought about that, it drove her wild. It turned her inside out. Betty couldn't get away from it. She and Dan had almost completely stopped going out together in public, and that only added to the panicky feeling that underneath it was all because of Linda.

Betty was hungry. It was a wild, ravenous, uncontrollable hunger for food, jewels, furs, clothes, anything that could fill the growing sense of emptiness. The hole in her heart that wouldn't go away. Anything to make herself feel she was still worth something. The closet was filling up with two-thousand-dollar outfits that she bought and never wore. She didn't even take the tags off. She was also gaining a lot of weight.

Sometimes looking for a house distracted her. There was no pleasing Dan. She just couldn't find a place he liked.

"There's a crack in the slab of our house," he announced one day. "The whole foundation is shaky. To get it fixed, we've got to tear the whole house apart. If we sell it this way, we'll take a huge loss. Let's rent a place. The insurance company will cover all the costs. Then, when the slab is fixed, we'll sell the house and buy another."

Betty believed him. She found a lovely rental home in La Jolla Shores owned by a very wealthy couple who lived in Denver and only used it in the summer. "It's perfect," she told Dan. "We can rent it for the school year."

On moving day Dan put his clothing and his shoes into the red Corvette. "I'm done," he said, and drove away. "We're moving four kids from a house we've been in for ten years and that's all you do to help," she said bitterly when he showed up the next day.

"I packed, you unpack." Then Betty got into her car and drove around for a few hours. It was the principle of the thing. She hated being walked on. She was changing. She wanted to show him how it felt. She was finally angry enough to strike back at the daily slights.

Her jaw was so tight, she had trouble opening her mouth. Betty went to the dentist. "It's tension, a hell of a lot of tension" he said. "What's the problem."

"I think Dan's having an affair with his secretary," she confided.

"You mean Linda?" he said.

"How did you know?"

"He sent her to see me to have her teeth fixed. She's beautiful but she's just a baby. Don't worry, you're terrific, and besides, you have all those nice kids. I'll talk to him."

November was the month of the Blackstone Ball, the biggest social event in town. Betty had spent months getting everything ready. A gorgeous Bob Mackie gown, shoes, stockings, earrings, purse, everything was perfect. She thought she looked great.

"I don't want to go," he said when she walked downstairs to present herself. "I don't love you anymore."

"Every time I get up, you knock me down," Betty said. She ran to the bathroom and locked the door. A few minutes later he was knocking. "Okay, I'll go," he yelled from the other side. It was too late. Her face was all blotched and swollen. She felt sick from the crying and the disappointment.

"I want to die," she told him through the door.

"Not tonight. Everyone's expecting us," he said. Betty fixed her makeup, and they went.

A few nights after that Dan came in late. He crawled into bed next to her. "Want to fuck," he whispered. Betty was lying on her back. She turned toward him. His breath smelled of alcohol. He reached out for her. He touched her lips with his fingers. His hands reeked of vaginal odor. She pushed him away. Betty had never smelled that smell before except on herself, and she knew he hadn't been near her. She wondered what had happened. Maybe Dan and Linda had fought. Maybe she had kicked him out of the house. Maybe it was just the memory of her that turned him on.

"You're so gross," Betty said. "You don't even wash your hands before coming home to me. You make me sick." The tears rolled down the sides of her face onto the pillow.

He reached for her breasts and climbed on top. "It's just you, just you. There is nobody else," he said. Betty felt trapped. If she rejected him, she'd be pushing him back to Linda. If she let him make love to her, she'd lose her self-respect. Sometimes she really thought he was driving her crazy on purpose.

• 10 •

Betty Broderick on Dan and Linda

"Linda would laugh with him when he was drunk and silly. She had no responsibilities at home. Dan and Linda would go out drinking, and she and he would both be drunk. She did not have to come home and be the mother to those four kids and get breakfast on the table and get them going. She had no responsibilities to anyone in life. I had a full slate of responsibilities. The girls were teenagers. They were the ones who you'd expect to be drunk and laughing in the bushes. But Dan and Linda were drunk and laughing in the bushes in the middle of the night, waking up my teenaged kids. There's something wrong with this picture, you know. I was trying to raise our children. I was trying to teach them don't fuck around and don't do drugs and don't get drunk. But how could I teach the children when Dan was acting like that himself, right?

"How can you tell your children don't do what I do? So, as my responsibilities grew and grew, I had to cover all the bases for Dan.

"Linda let him do whatever he wanted to do. She had to. If she stood up to him and said, 'Why are you drunk?' she'd be replaced in a minute. Part of the deal was that she would adore him and approve of everything he did. What did she have to lose? I said that to Dan Broderick at a very sober time when I was talking to him. I said, 'Everyone whose last name is Broderick is going to lose in this.'

"All of us had everything to lose and nothing to gain by him marrying Linda Kolkena. He was ruining my kids' future, my kids' lives, my future, his own future. He was never again going to be the outstanding citizen he painted himself as being.

"I said, 'Dan, look at your friends who have done this. Who have left their wives and their children and married these young girls. Not one of them is happy. Not one of them. They've left their wife and kids. The kids all drop out of school, the wives all get depressed. They never last with the young girl, it never works. And then you can't go back and repair it.'

"He didn't want to grow up. He refused to mature. He wanted to be young again. He wanted to enjoy his money because when we were young, we didn't have it. That's why I always said he went through typical mid-life crisis. He was the perfect candidate. I told him that he was the cover of Mid-life Crisis magazine with the girlfriend and the red Corvette and leather jacket and the *Risky Business* sunglasses. I said, 'Dan, you're playing a joke on me. This is funny. You're just doing this to me to be funny, right? You're a caricature of a forty-year-old man.' Right on schedule. He was so busy working through school and everything that he didn't enjoy his youth. Now he had money and he wanted to go back and live his youth over again. He did not want a houseful of children and expenses and bills. He wanted to be young and free and rich. Wouldn't we all?"

• 11 •

Dan's fortieth birthday was coming up. Betty was so glad that they were still together in the rental house and so full of hope that she invited his family from all over the country with their spouses and all their kids for a five-day birthday celebration.

His birthday was on Thursday, Thanksgiving Day. Everyone flew in on Wednesday.

Betty sold her own stocks to pay for it. She rented all the hotel rooms at the Colonial Inn in La Jolla. She organized all the dinners, all the lunches, all the breakfasts, and hired all the baby-sitters. It was all set up with prewritten checks stapled to the receipts. The only thing she couldn't control was the weather. She had rented buses, rented cars, and arranged the food. Everything worked smoothly, no glitches. Many of these people had never been to California, so it was very exciting.

Betty presented them with a printed itinerary of what they were going to do while they were visiting. She picked them up at the airport and shuttled them back and forth to the Colonial Inn. It was a lovely hotel, with a fireplace and a big living room, just small enough so that they could basically take over the place and not be obnoxious. She brought the families in there one by one as they arrived. The first night they all had dinner at El Pescador, a fish place with big, long tables. The next morning was Thanksgiving Day. They went to the beach near the house and had sodas and beer and hors d'oeuvres and played football on the grass.

There were about forty people, from little tiny kids to grandpas. After the beach they went to the hotel, where they had a private dining room with a big L-shaped table. They ate turkey, did toasts, took pictures.

On Friday they did the grand tour of San Diego. Betty hired little buses called people movers. They all got on the people movers and went to the San Diego Zoo and to Old Town. It was like a professional tour of all the stops in San Diego. Then they went down to the water and took a harbor cruise. They had a wonderful time. That night they ate a catered Mexican dinner in the courtyard of the rental house. Dan even agreed to let Betty invite some of his legal friends and their wives.

The next morning they chartered a giant bus to Los Angeles to see the USC–Notre Dame football game. Betty arranged for deli sand-wiches, croissants, Danishes, hot coffee, and Bloody Marys on the way up.

Nothing was too good for Dan's family. Betty the perfectionist had planned another flawless weekend.

Christmas 1984, there was no party again. The children loved the rental house. Betty decorated it very nicely. Each child had a wish list on the refrigerator and each child got everything on the list. Kim and Lee each got a suitcase with wheels and a Eurorail Pass. Rhett got a huge Care-Bear and Danny got a real puppy. Betty told Dan that this year for Christmas she wanted a ring from the Collection, a fancy jewelry store in La Jolla. It was a gorgeous emerald-diamond ring. She showed him a picture of it in a San Diego magazine.

They could easily afford it. It was something her friends would notice, especially the ones who'd been calling her with reports about Linda.

Betty had wanted that ring for a year. They were traveling with a crowd where the women all had diamond Rolex watches and fancy jewelry. It was a very lovely and expensive ring, but not big or gaudy or flashy.

She could have bought it for herself. That wasn't the point. Betty wanted a sign of recommitment from Dan. Something that said I know you've gone through hell, even though I've never fessed up to it. She wanted a truce and a promise.

A lot of Dan's friends had done the same things to their wives, then gone back and given them major trips or major cars or major furs as a gift of love. A gift that said, "I'm here to stay, and this seals it. I've been a rat, but it's behind us now."

That ring would mean to Betty that Linda wasn't really important. That after all the dust settled, Betty was the wife, and after twenty years together she still came first. It would, she thought, help erase some of the bad feelings, the loneliness, the sense of loss. Sometimes Betty felt like a kid pulling petals off a daisy—"He loves me, he loves me not." It wasn't so much the ring she wanted. It was the proof. It was that last petal saying, "Yes, I'm here and I love you."

On Christmas morning Dan handed Betty a box. She had already spotted it under the tree. She picked it up and turned it over. She could hardly wait to open it. When she finally did, Betty felt as if she'd been socked. It looked like a child's ring. Both the stone and the ring were too small for her, like something for a six-year-old. To her that meant he didn't care. She wondered if Linda had gotten the real one.

"This is an insult," she said. "Keep it. I wouldn't be caught dead wearing this. It's not even worth the gas to take it back. It's a piece of shit." Betty felt like a real bitch. She knew that the ring wasn't the most important thing in the world. She knew she was setting a lousy example for the kids, but she couldn't help it. She had bet Dan's love on that ring, and lost.

• 13 •

Linda loved the new life-style. Since Dan had come into her world, she'd gone from renting a room under the jet path in Point Loma to jewels, expensive furs, and a new car. Now Dan was helping her buy a condo. Cosigning, he liked to say. Still, Dan was married, and Linda was restless.

She missed Dan so much at night that she found other lovers. She was tired of being the mistress in Dan's life. Still, it wasn't all bad. Linda liked the freedom. She enjoyed shopping for her own condo and making her own decisions.

Now as she walked into the living room of a new model condo, a young man with a square jaw and sandy hair caught her eye. Linda smiled. The handsome young man smiled. The attraction was instant, for both of them. Steve Kelly was struck not only by Linda's beauty but also by her manner. Most of the best-looking women he knew weren't funny and smart. He could tell Linda was someone he could laugh with. He also knew right away that she was someone he'd love to touch.

After the first twenty minutes Steve Kelly went home and told his roommate he had just met "the" girl. She was, he said, an absolutely perfect woman.

For the next three months they saw each other every night. It was very intense, very passionate, a real closeness. For a while they even lived together. Linda's condo was ready before Steve's, and he had already given notice.

Linda made sure Dan knew that she was seeing Steve and a couple of other guys too. It was the leverage that she had. After all, he was still married. But it was harder during those long, passionate nights with Steve to admit to him that she was also sleeping with her boss.

Linda didn't exactly think it out. She just started letting Steve know in increments, giving out little clues, and talking about Dan a lot.

In her own way she loved them both. Steve was gorgeous and smart and talented, but he was just a kid starting out, a Dartmouth graduate who'd majored in English and landed his first job as a political cartoonist at the *San Diego Union*. He wasn't a star like Dan Broderick. An M.D., a Harvard-trained lawyer, and a millionaire. Steve couldn't begin to give Linda the things that Dan was already providing.

She wanted children, status, a beautiful home, and a rich, smart husband. She didn't want to start out at the Laundromat. She didn't want to spend twenty years helping someone build a life. She didn't have to. Dan Broderick had it all.

The more Linda raved about her boss, the more it became a sensitive point with Steve Kelly. "If he's so perfect, why aren't you with him?" Steve finally asked.

"He's married with four kids. We'd never do that," she insisted. For a long time Steve accepted it. When you love a woman as much as Steve loved Linda, it's easy to live in denial.

Then she took him up to the office. After that he had a hard time fooling himself. To Steve this looked like the office of a high-powered executive complete with lavish furniture, an elaborate stereo system, and floor-to-ceiling windows overlooking the San Diego waterfront. But Linda was a kid who couldn't type and had never even finished high school.

Steve began to wonder if she was lying to him. He began to doubt her integrity. He casually questioned her on a number of occasions.

For example, he was curious when Dan went away on business and left her his red Corvette. He asked again when a dozen long-stemmed red roses arrived from Dan on her birthday while he was away in Europe. Then a few days later a color television set was delivered as a gift. Linda always said it was nothing.

When she showed up three hours late for a date, Steve confronted her directly. This time Linda cried and admitted that they had once been lovers, but swore that they had ended it. "Okay," Steve said. "I can live with that."

Once Linda got started crying and talking about the past, it was hard to calm her down. She just kept bawling her eyes out, remembering the time she had been date-raped when she was still in high school. It was a story that might have reminded Betty of her wedding night, but Steve had no associations. He just put his arms around her. There were times, he figured, when a woman needed some comfort.

After that there was always tension between them, a nagging question in Steve's mind about Linda's character. He'd never been lied to before by a woman. He'd never been betrayed. It made him jealous and suspicious. He didn't blame Linda for being attracted to Dan. He could see that in some ways they were right for each other. That only made it worse.

Steve went away to San Francisco for a few days. He came back to a confession. "While you were gone," Linda said, "I slept with Dan, but now it's really over."

"This time," Steve said, "I'd like to hear that from him." Reluctantly Linda arranged for Steve to come into the inner sanctum and meet Dan Broderick face-to-face.

"I know this is awkward," Steve told Dan from across the desk, "but I need to hear from you that what Linda tells me is true, that from now on you and she are only going to work professionally and not be involved."

"Yeah," Dan said without looking up. "No problem." He was very cold, not sympathetic at all. Linda ushered Steve out. After that they got into some pretty heated discussions. Not just about Linda sleeping with Dan, but about morality in general.

"Linda," Steve said, "you've come between two people with four children. Let them try to get their lives back together." She was silent. "What you did was wrong. It was reckless. It's okay to make a mistake, but now correct it. Leave the job, go back to school, or get another job. I'll put you through school if you want to go. You can build your own career. As long as you work for him, there will be something between you and Dan."

"No," Linda said. "I like my job. I can stay where I am and not sleep with him. Betty ought to be able to handle that."

"Well, she can't," Steve said, getting angry. "You're driving her crazy. If you and Dan want to get married and live happily ever after, then do it right. Let him leave her and divorce her first. Don't keep rubbing her face in it."

A big trial was coming up in Palm Springs. Linda wanted to go with Dan. "We'll have separate hotel rooms," Linda said. They argued about that trip for a month. Steve still thought that they were really sleeping together. Finally he said, "If you go, we're finished. I'm starting to understand how Betty feels. I can't handle it anymore either."

He convinced her that she needed an objective opinion from a third person. He took her to see a therapist, a lady over at the University Towne Centre, upstairs above the bank building. Steve was hoping she'd be talked out of going to Palm Springs and having an affair with a married man with four children. Instead the therapist told Linda to go with her instincts. Linda followed the instructions. She turned around and gave Dan Broderick an ultimatum.

"It's me or your wife," she said. "Make your choice."

• 14 •

Betty Broderick on the Affair with Linda

"I knew it was happening and I asked Dan about it. I said, 'I have no money, I have no account, I have nothing, but you're paying Linda all this money, plus you buy her a car, you buy her a condo, you're paying off all her clothes, all her dinners, and she's getting paid.'

"I knew that she had a new condominium, a brand-new Toyota convertible, a fur coat, and very expensive clothes. And I knew that when he met her, she had zip, zero, nothing, and her family had zip, zero, nothing.

"People would call me and say, 'She was walking around town with a MasterCard that said "Daniel T. Broderick" on line one and "Linda Kolkena" on line two, and those bills went to the office. I also found one of the receipts. I flipped out. I was married to him. I had no credit card that said him and me on it. He was paying all those bills. When I confronted him, he took out his checkbook and wrote me a twenty-five-thousand-dollar check. I never touched it. I didn't want Dan Broderick's money. I just wanted him to understand where I was coming from. His money was my money. I just wanted to make a point. There was nothing I wanted with twenty-five thousand dollars anyway. It was just the principle of the thing.

"I called him every name in the book, but I never called him dumb. He owned her. He literally owned everything about her, which was just the way he liked his women. They could never leave him or walk out on him. He owned her job, her car, her apartment, everything. Perfect for him. She was willing to put up with all his shit, and she was happy to be owned. Her sister said, 'Linda wants children,' and I said, 'Great, don't we all. But if you meet someone else's husband, they already have children.'

"Go out and find a nice young husband like Steve Kelly, and put in your twenty years going up the ladder. It's okay if she just wanted to have children, but there are ways to do it.

"Dan really didn't want to divorce me either. He slept with me all the time. I mean like at least three or four times a week all through Linda. He learned some new tricks from her. Until then it was simply the missionary position. One, two, three, no foreplay. I had no one to compare him with. I had no frame of reference. I'd never had any other lover. But Linda was experienced and she must have been demanding things. At a paperback bookstore he bought a book on the G-spot. He sat there reading it right in front of me.

"A strange benefit of his being with Linda is that he had actually become a better lover to me. I was the beneficiary there for a while. It was a tremendous improvement. I thought it was ironic. He was trying everything out on me. If I hadn't known why it was happening, I'd have thought it was great. I knew right away it was different. Everything else was falling apart, and our sex life was getting better and better. The new passion, the lovemaking, drew me closer. It was really strange, pleasurable, and painful at the same time."

• 15 •

On February 28, 1985, Betty was lying in bed watching the news. Dan came home late. The kids were asleep. He walked over to the antique armoire and opened it. "I'm leaving," he said.

"Where are you going?" Betty asked, flipping the channel with the remote control. She thought he was going to the 7-Eleven or something.

"I'm moving out. I'm not happy," he answered. He started carrying his clothes out to the red Corvette. Suddenly Betty was alert, agitated, she felt the old sharp tightening in the lower half of her stomach.

They'd fight and make up and fight and make up, he'd get rude, then she'd get defensive and be rude back, but he had never moved out of the house before.

"What the hell's happening now?" she said. He ignored her. The tight, aching feeling was moving up into her chest. She was trying to control herself. When the clothes were in the car, he came back up.

"So," she said, "you're just leaving for the rest of the marriage. What about me. What about the kids? What are we supposed to do?"

"Frankly, my dear," he said. "I don't give a damn."

They stared at each other.

"Who the hell do you think you are? This isn't *Gone With the Wind*. I can't turn it off and go home."

From across the room, from ten feet away, she could feel his anger.

"Why don't you just call your friend Roger?" he spat.

"My friend Roger. Who the hell is Roger?"

"You know, Roger Zucchet, that architect friend of yours. You really enjoyed dancing with him, didn't you?"

Betty looked at him. "This is bizarre," she said. "This is perverted. That was two years ago, at a public street party with thousands of people dancing in the street and you right there. Nothing happened. I'm not that type. Everybody was dancing with everybody else, except you because you don't dance.

"Yeah, Roger Zucchet's good-looking and I was good-looking too. We made a great looking couple in that picture in the *La Jolla Light*, but I can't believe that this has been eating away at you. I can't believe you've been pissed off about this for two years. You're jealous and you never said a word." Her face softened. She smiled and walked toward him and put her hands on his shoulders.

"Do you want me to leave now or in the morning," he asked.

"I've been married to a lawyer too long to answer that question," she said. He put his arms around her.

"I just need some space, Betts. I need some time."

"Is it Linda?" she asked.

"No," Dan answered. "Linda has nothing to do with this. Come on," he whispered, kissing her.

She wanted to hold him again and make it all disappear. They climbed into bed.

"Oh, God," she thought. "What's next?"

In the morning he didn't say anything. Not even good-bye. Just got up and left in his red Corvette while she was still asleep.

• 16 •

Betty cried a lot. Sometimes she screamed. She told herself he was coming back, and that kept her going. She and the kids stayed in the rental house in La Jolla Shores. She tried to pretend nothing was wrong. Mighty Mouse, she called herself. She didn't want the kids to be as scared as she was.

They went to Warner Springs Ranch, which they owned with another couple, to get away from it all. That's when the rats invaded the rental house. The prince walks out. The rats take over. A fairy tale gone bad. Only this was no fairy tale, it was very real. The house had a crawl space underneath. Someone had cut square holes in the space where round pipes went through for the washer and dryer. The rats were sliding in through the spaces. They were all over the place. In the refrigerator, in the beds, in the closets. It was incredible. Betty had never seen anything like it.

"It's okay, don't be scared, I'll take care of everything, I'll call the people," she told the kids. Meanwhile the rats ate the stuffing out of the back of the couch. She could hear them in the closets at night. They shredded her long gowns. Her ring disappeared from the counter. "Rats like shiny things," Danny explained.

Betty was still trying to cover up. "We're just giving Daddy some space," she said lightly. "He's staying at the other house while the workmen fix it. I'm taking care of you kids over here and I'm taking care of the rats. I'm in charge here. Everything is fine." She had no idea how she was going to pay the bills. She didn't know if Dan was going to visit on the weekends or if he was even going to call again.

Finally Betty picked up the phone, once again turning to him for help and not dealing with the reality of his indifference. "Dan," she said. "I'm sorry to bother you at work, but I'm really scared. You've got to come over here and help. There are rats everywhere. All the traps are snapping. They're full. Every trap has a rat in it, and it's not even dark yet."

"Congratulations," he said, and hung up.

When the phone clicked, Betty got hysterical. She ran out of the kitchen. The first thing she saw was a half-dead rat in a trap in the laundry room. She began crying. Lee tried to help. She got a shovel and pushed the rat into a bucket of water to drown it. When Kim saw that, she started screaming and fighting with Lee. "Cut this shit out," Betty yelled. By now she was an absolute wreck. Kim still wouldn't stop.

"Okay, that's it. You're going to Daddy's. Get your stuff." She couldn't pretend she was handling it anymore. Dan would have to help. If not with the rats, then with the kids. Betty dropped Kim off at their old house, where Dan was living alone.

The next day when Danny began to fight with Rhett, she took Danny. She was hurt and she was angry. She wanted Dan to get involved, to help with these problems. *Let him find out what it's like to manage these kids by himself,* she thought. *Then he'll want me back.* It seemed like the perfect way to make him realize how much he needed her. How much they all needed each other.

She had always left him insulated because he had so much stress at work. Look what it led to. She told herself, *This can't be happening. It's only temporary. Just a mid-life crisis.* It was three months after his fortieth birthday. All the books told her not to become a nagging mother figure. But what was she supposed to do? There was no understanding between them, about getting back together or not getting back together, about the children, about the house, about the money. He was just doing whatever he wanted. The night she dropped Danny off, Dan finally called. *Thank God,* she thought when she heard his voice. *It's working.*

91

"We'll be sticking to the terms of the original lease. You'll have to be out in June," he said.

"What?" she screamed. "We have to talk. Where am I supposed to go? I don't know what's going on. I can't live like this. I have no idea about money. You know I don't do money. I always gave you my paycheck. I've never paid rent in my life. I've never even asked how much anything cost. My mom and dad paid for everything before I married you. I have no idea of taxes or house payments or phone bills or anything. I'm absolutely sheltered, absolutely unprepared."

He came over. "Dan, I need guidelines," she said. I'm begging you." He smiled.

"Don't worry, we'll work it out," he said soothingly. "We're not getting divorced, we're buying a house. We're getting back together. Have you been looking for a house like you're supposed to?"

"Yes," she said. "I have been looking. As a matter of fact I found a place. It's on Calle del Cielo. The house is a tear down, but the site is terrific. It has a cul-de-sac with a gorgeous view of the ocean. We could build anything we want on it."

"Okay," he said. "We'll take a look at it."

Then, just like old times, they were back in bed.

• 17 •

Dan liked the land. "We'll buy it," he said. The closing was delayed, and Betty had to get out of the rental. The logical thing to do was to move back in with Dan. All the kids were there. She had brought Rhett and Lee over when she went to her father's seventy-fifth birthday party in New York the week before.

While she was visiting, she had also broken the news to her parents. "Dan's having a mid-life crisis. He's sleeping with his secretary," she said. "But don't worry, we're working it out. We're not getting divorced." They seemed relieved.

Betty came over to Dan's with her stuff.

"Thank God, we're finally all together again," she said. "The kids are back in their own rooms. They have their friends again, they're secure, they're happy."

"I need some space," Dan announced about five days later. They had just signed the new sales agreement. "I want you to stay at the new house for a while. Get it ready for the architect. I'll take care of the kids and everything here."

Betty was still hoping to please him, still trying to be the good little girl. She kissed the kids, packed a suitcase and a sleeping bag, and went to the empty house. She lay down on the floor and stared up at the ceiling. She got up and walked to the window and watched the sunset. Suddenly she was sweating. She tried to look at her watch. The sweat made it slide around on her arm. The room was dirty and hot. Her teeth chattered. Her muscles tightened. She lay down on the floor without a pillow or a sheet. Then she was shaking. The sunset reminded her of the day she went to Dan's office and sat there waiting for him until the sunset, then went home and burned the clothes.

Suddenly she began throwing up and sobbing. It went on like that for days. The depression got so bad, she couldn't lift her arms, couldn't hold her body up. She was slumped over, walking around holding on to the walls, tired all the time, but unable to sleep.

Slowly she began to come out of it. *This is only temporary,* she told herself. *Just till Dan gets finished fucking Linda. I'll let him do it,* she decided. "Get it out of your system, honey," she said out loud. "Fucking Linda isn't worth throwing away the family. There are six people in this family. If that's what your mid-life crisis is, go ahead, fuck her. But then come back to us and let's get on with our lives."

After a while she convinced herself they'd all be together again soon. She began to look around at the empty house and think about the future. The house had been on the market for two years. The rugs were filthy. There were no appliances in the kitchen. Holes were in the floor. Every bedroom door had literally been kicked. It was a mess. It had three bedrooms, but the people who owned it had marketed it as an eight-bedroom rental. They put walls or curtains down the middle of two bedrooms, then turned the garage into three more bedrooms. The garage still had the garage doors. It had no windows or closets. They only got away with it because it was on the beach.

There was every kind of damage in that house, including termites and rats inside and out.

Betty tried to energize herself. All the furniture and all her clothes were at the other house. No point in bringing anything over. They were supposed to tear the place down any day. All Don Edson, the architect, needed was a soils engineer to test the soil. All Betty needed was a five-thousand-dollar check.

"Let's not do it right now," Dan said. "I have a cash crunch with buying the house and the down payment. Let's just wait a little while."

Suddenly everything was on hold. Betty knew she wasn't welcome at the house. The kids were safe. There was nothing for her to do. So she took a weekend trip. When she got back, her things had been moved into the garage. The maid Dan hired met her at the door wearing her clothes. "Your husband gave me your bed and your clothes. He said I could have the rest of the stuff in the garage," she said, pointing to Betty's belongings. "He said it was all junk."

"He did?" Betty stammered. She could hardly believe it. "I'm sorry, but those are all my things, they're not throwaways. I mean, that's everything I own, that's my real stuff, not the excess. I'm living in an empty house with one suitcase and no bed and no furniture. I need those things."

Then Betty found out that the kids weren't even there. They had been sent off to Gold Arrow Camp while she was away. It was a good camp, they'd been there before. But Dan had made the arrangements without consulting her. He deliberately kept it from her. He even kept it from the kids until the last weekend so that they wouldn't tell her. Betty found the application form. In case of emergency if Dan couldn't be reached, it said, the camp should call Dan's brother, Larry, in Colorado. "My God," she thought, "it's as if I'm dead and the kids don't have a mother."

At that, Betty got frightened. She knew no way to stop Dan. The more she thought about it, the more afraid she became. She tried to calm herself by putting it out of her thoughts.

94

She still couldn't face the truth. She just kept on getting all these estimates and interviewing contractors and builders. She had a huge file. She was waiting for the kids to come back from camp. Instead Dan sent them directly to his parents' house in Ohio. He bought the tickets and had them put on the plane. Never even asked her.

Betty was devastated. She was tired of living in the unlivable house. She didn't know what to do with herself. Finally she pulled herself together. She called a travel agent. "I always wanted to see Vancouver, British Columbia, and Victoria Island," she said. Betty ended up with a group of old people on a tour. They were all ninety-nine years old. She didn't know anybody. Brian Birchill drove the tour bus. Betty struck up a conversation with him. She was unused to being on her own and not part of a couple—but she didn't want to be defeated. She didn't want to let it ruin his life. "I think I'll skip dinner. I'll rent a bike and ride around," she said.

"Would you mind if I rented a bike, too, and came with you?" he asked.

"Hell, no," she answered. "You live here, you can show me around. So they rode their bikes all over and had a great time. He was a shy, sensitive kind man.

When Betty said good-bye to him, she held out her hand. "Thank you," she said. "Now I owe you. If you ever come to San Diego, I'll give you a tour. I've got a big house. You can even stay with me."

"I'm going to take you up on that," Brian answered.

• 18 •

The minute she heard the kids were there Betty went over to Dan's house.

Rhett's head was shaven. He was practically bald. "Oh, my God," Betty said. "I bet Grandpa did it. Where was Grandma?"

"She was crying in the corner, saying, 'Don't do it, don't do it,' but Grampa wouldn't stop. He just shaved my whole head."

"Crying in the corner? I would have used chairs and baseball bats. I would have taken my shoe off and beat the old man on the head." She swept Rhett up in her arms and kissed him.

"Grampa told Daddy and Uncle Larry he was going to do it when they left."

" 'If you touch my son,' " Uncle Larry said, " 'I will burn your house to the ground.' "

"Daddy just said, 'Please, don't do it.' So when they left, Grampa grabbed me. He held me on the ground."

"Never mind, honey," Betty said. "It'll grow back. He's just an old man." *An old man in conflict with his sons,* she thought. *When the sons get bigger and the father stops beating them, he has to find someone little to pick on.*

Years ago Betty had heard that the old man had had to buy a Cadillac just so that he could drive by his own father's house and show him that he was more successful. It was a major goal in his life to outdo his own father. Now Dan had the same goal.

Thank God at least the kids were finally home. Betty ran around the house hugging them. She just couldn't get enough, especially of Rhett because he had been hurt. She followed him down to the kitchen, asking a million questions.

There was a sloppy-looking Boston cream pie sitting on the counter. Just like the ones she used to make for Dan when they were dating, only a lot messier. She figured one of the kids had been baking.

"Who made that?" she asked, smiling. Danny frowned.

"Linda," the new maid answered. "She brought it over for Dan when she visited last night."

"Oh, that's nice," Betty said. She didn't know what else to say. She must have made a thousand for him over the years. *Fuck you. Pow on you, buddy,* she thought. Betty could feel the pain behind her eyes. It was the same kind of cream pie she used to make when they were dating and first got married. He was playing the same game with

Linda, exactly the same, but she didn't know it. Betty was the only one who knew he'd done all this before.

A country-western song was going through her head, but she couldn't exactly remember the words. "He says the same things to me." Eyeball to eyeball he'd told her he never slept with Linda. That she was losing it, that she was crazy. And he was sleeping with both of them on the very same day.

Betty picked up the pie and carried it upstairs—into the master bedroom. She looked at the neatly made king-size bed and thought of them doing it, with her kids asleep in the next room. Her beautiful children, her beautiful house.

"So, nothing's going on with the cunt," she said as she threw the pie onto the bed. She picked up the pan and smeared the cream and the chocolate all over the covers and all over Dan's cashmere sweaters. Then she went into the bathroom and washed her hands.

• 19 •

Betty wandered around alone in the sand dunes. A chill came in. The wind blew, and she thought again of the old days, of Dan walking with her. She remembered how, when they were alone, he would put his arms around her and how their bodies were drawn together like magnets. These days a lot of the past was locked up inside her.

She clung to the memory of old love and the way they had lived as a family, especially the memory of the holidays. She still had that practical side. After all, Betty was a teacher and a mother. She lived for Halloween, Thanksgiving, and Christmas and for all the birthdays and holidays in between that were family traditions.

October 28th was coming up. That was Octoberfest at Larry's. From there every year they'd always go on to Notre Dame and watch the game that marked the weekend they first met. It had been going on every year for seventeen years. This year Dan was taking the kids and going to Larry's without her.

Betty decided to go to the Bishop School fashion show and luncheon. At least it would give her some place to be on October 28th. It was an enormous effort just to get dressed and into the car. Talking to people and acting happy would be even harder.

"Hi, Irene. You look so cute," Betty called, waving cheerfully to another mother from across the room. It took Irene almost a minute to figure out that it was Betty.

"Just look at me, just look at what he's done to me," Betty said as soon as she saw the shocked look on Irene's face. Irene looked. Betty's clothes were very expensive, a beautiful orange outfit, but her face was bloated and broken out, her eyes were swollen. She was much heavier. Her makeup was too thick. She was trying too hard to smile. "It's been a very difficult summer," Betty admitted.

When Betty got home, her sister-in-law, Kathy, called. "Dan came to the Octoberfest with his secretary, Linda," she said. Once again Betty felt as if death had called. If it came now, it would be a welcome relief.

The next night Dan came to the house and opened the door with his key. "What's your explanation this time?" Betty asked sarcastically. "I know you always have an explanation for everything you do with Linda. Did she just happen to get on the same plane? Did she just happen to wander into our family party?"

"Betty," Dan said. "I've come over here to tell you something very specific. You were right all along. I've been having an affair with Linda for three years."

Betty began to shake. She sat on the floor in her robe and slippers and watched the room turn dark. Suddenly she got up and walked toward him. She began hitting him with her fists. He grabbed her hands and held her down. He wouldn't let go. "You're sick, you're crazy, you need help. Get dressed," he ordered, "I'm taking you to a mental institution and having you committed."

"Bullshit, you motherfuckin' son of a bitch," she shouted. "I loved you, I trusted you. Yes, I'm upset, I'm very upset. You've been lying to me for three years, you son of a bitch, but that doesn't mean I'm sick."

"Your illness is what caused me to be with Linda in the first place," he said, still holding her down. Betty stopped struggling. She closed her eyes. She was trying not to pass out. It was all coming back to her in a rush. There was a certain satisfaction in knowing she'd been right all along, but it cut deeper than the razor on her wrist ever had. She saw Dan's office again, the streamers, the half-eaten chocolate-mousse cake. The terrifying emptiness was back. She could see the sun setting, and now she could also see an image of Dan and Linda in bed, laughing. The only man she'd ever loved and trusted screwing this girl who looked like she had looked seventeen years ago. She clenched her fist, tearing the skin of her own palm with her nails and staring into Dan's eyes. "You picked the right girl to marry, but the wrong girl to fuck," she said.

Misery was what she felt, misery and loss. He stared back at her. There was a strange, sad grin on his face. It frightened her. She shut her eyes again. As soon as she did, the image of Dan and Linda came back. "All these years you've been fucking that cunt and lying to me," she moaned. Then they were both silent. It was so quiet that they could hear the waves hitting the sand. She felt like that sand, like the dirt under his feet.

"What I've done I can't undo," he said finally.

"I was right all along. With every instinct I knew I was right, and you kept telling me I was crazy," she said. "Even when I smelled the cunt on your hands, you denied it. You want me to be crazy, to justify what you've done." The last of her sadness was turning to rage. "And if I wasn't crazy, you'd make me crazy by betraying me over and over, because it's easier to leave a crazy wife than a good one who still loves you. You do everything you can to see that I never get my balance.

"Whenever I believed you were finished with Linda, you made sure I heard about a party or a lunch date or a weekend trip. You did whatever it took to keep me guessing, to make me scream, to keep me out of control. You told our kids that I was crazy, but you know I'm not crazy, except to believe your lies again and again for so long."

Betty got up and walked into the bedroom. She could hear him pick up the telephone and dial.

"She won't come," Dan whispered into the phone. "Tell the doctor my wife refuses to be committed."

Son of a bitch, she thought. *He even had that planned.*

"I want to go home, Dan," she said, opening the bedroom door. "I want to see my kids. I want to sleep in my own bed. I've been sleeping on the floor long enough."

Dan looked at her as if everything inside him hurt. Then he held out his hand. "Come," he said, "I'll take you home."

PART IV

• • •

Fury

"It won't be over till one of us is dead."

—Dan Broderick, 1989

• 1 •

She had just come back to the empty house.

"Something here for you, ma'am," a man in a sheriff's uniform said, holding up a large envelope.

From the corner of her eye Betty could see Dan's return address.

"Your husband wanted you served at the Bishop School luncheon," the man said. "But I couldn't locate you there among all those ladies, and I've got to serve you directly. It's the law."

"Son of a bitch," she said as she opened the envelope. "Divorce papers. Oh, my God, divorce papers. He was trying to serve me there to humiliate me."

Betty remembered Dan laughing with delight when he had thought of similar things to do with his lawsuits. He actually used to lie in bed nights thinking these things up. Nastygrams, he called them. Once he served a doctor in the front row of his parish on Christmas Eve. Dan thought that was a riot. The doctor was some sort of elder in his church. Dan sent the marshal there deliberately to humiliate him in front of his family and friends.

Betty felt weary, beaten down. She remembered the look she had seen reflected in other people's eyes when Dan took them on. This time it was in her eyes. Pain flashed from one side of her temple to the other.

Dan would attack her now just as he would any other adversary, someone he planned to crush. That's what he did best. That's how he made a million a year before he was forty. It would be worse with her. He'd have a personal vendetta. *Ironic,* she thought. *I stood behind him admiring his increasing skill, his killer instinct, his success-at-any-cost philosophy. During all those years I never thought I'd be at the receiving end.*

Fear quickened her pulse rate. She could feel her heart pounding.

103

She could actually see her chest thumping. Finally the light dawned. *A lawyer,* she thought. *I need to find the best lawyer there is.*

Sitting by the phone with the San Diego book in her lap, Betty started calling the ten top divorce lawyers in town. After number five it dawned on her that this was never going to work. They wouldn't take a case against Dan Broderick. He was too powerful. He was a tremendous source of referrals for them. None of them wanted to go against him. Since 1983 Dan had been cultivating these friendships. He was also aligning himself to be the next president of the San Diego County Bar Association. Every lawyer and judge in town knew that. They were all members.

The sixth lawyer, who was also her friend, said, "Betty, you're going to have to go out of town. No one here will touch it." Betty knew right away that any L.A. lawyer would be at a huge disadvantage in a San Diego courtroom. If he was good, he'd have plenty of business in his own community. Why would he come to San Diego and be a little fish? "God," Betty said. "I don't even want a divorce. Now I have to drive three hours just to get a second-rate attorney."

"I'll call Ron Jaffe for you in L.A.," her friend said. "He's good. I think he'll do it for us."

Jaffe made it clear from the start that he didn't really want the case. He had more clients than he could handle in his own courthouse, where he knew all the ropes and the judges. He wasn't crazy about having to travel either.

The cost was going to be enormous. His estimate for her side alone was over one hundred thousand dollars. It seemed like a colossal waste of common property. "Why couldn't we just draw up a proposal and submit it?" she asked. "I have no interest in ripping Dan off or dragging him through the mud. I don't even need half. I want this over with as quickly and quietly as possible. I want a chunk in the bank for my old age and a monthly allowance I can live on." Those were the words, but the feelings were different. She couldn't bear the loss. Without Dan they weren't a family. More than anything she wanted to keep Dan with them. Maybe if she gave him the kids, he'd realize he couldn't manage alone either. He'd see how important she was.

"My house is unlivable for the kids or for me. I'm at a total loss as to whether I'll have to work or not." She said that for the time being the kids are all right where they are in their own house with all their things and their friends. "I talk to them everyday. I'm still the soccer coach and the room mother."

"Fine," Jaffe said. "Don't go to work, and don't sign anything."

Betty nodded. Jaffe pushed a very intimidating-looking agreement across the desk. It said his fee was $250 an hour, and $10,000 to get started. "I meant don't sign anything except this," he said, smiling.

"I don't have ten thousand beans," Betty told him.

"That's usually the case with the wife. Don't worry. I'll get it from Dan."

Jaffe sent off a letter requesting the $10,000 so that he could become the official attorney of record. Months passed. The check from Dan never came.

"I feel like killing the son of a bitch," Betty said when Jaffe called to tell her that he was still waiting for the money. "Did you ever feel like killing someone?" she repeated when he didn't respond.

"You're not serious, are you?" Jaffe said.

"No," she answered, "I'm kidding!"

• 2 •

Brian Birchill was taking a vacation. He wanted to see her. Betty figured it would take her mind off Dan. He came for dinner and stayed for breakfast. Brian camped at one end of the house and she camped at the other. It went on that way for two weeks. He was really nice. He helped her build a rose garden in the backyard. But Betty didn't get involved. She wanted to see what was happening with her real family. She wasn't looking for a boyfriend.

"Brian, I just can't." She finally told him. "I like you, I really do. But I'm still committed. I'm still waiting to see if I'll get back with Dan."

Betty had one comfort. Dan finally said the kids could come to visit. She bought fresh fruit and special food. She spent the entire day baking and cooking. There was so much bread in the oven and food on the counters that it looked like she was expecting the entire Marine Corps. "I forget what they like best," she told Brian.

Dan called on the day of the visit. "My plans changed," he said. "They're not coming."

The next day Betty went to school to pick them up as scheduled. When she got there, a maid or somebody had already taken them. She came home that night and cried. She just couldn't stop.

"You're crying all the time," Maria Montez said in broken English. "Crying in the morning, crying in the afternoon, and crying at night. Stop crying. The children will call, the children will come."

The children did call. They were crying too. They told her they missed her and that Daddy wouldn't let them come. That only made it worse. She spent the whole night crying. Brian was still there, but he was a stranger.

A stack of letters arrived. Each one was almost the same, but the addresses were different. They were all very legal and very proper. They all said that Dan Broderick had notified them that he was no longer legally responsible for any debts incurred by his wife, Betty Broderick.

The only other source of money she had now, besides what Dan chose to give her each month, was a checking account, and it was already overdrawn by $2,500. A few days later the phone rang. It was around eleven o'clock at night.

"Betty," Dan said. She could tell he'd been drinking. "I'm at Notre Dame at a game with Linda. Did you know it was twenty years ago tonight that we met? God, how I loved you. How beautiful you were. Remember all the good times we had?"

Betty rolled her eyes. She couldn't believe it. She took the receiver away from her ear and held it out so that Brian could hear. If she hadn't had someone there with her when that call came in, she would have thought she dreamed it.

106

• 3 •

Betty was the soccer coach for Rhett's team. She'd done the same for Danny. Without a parent participating in some way, a child couldn't join. The La Jolla Stringers was a little team, young boys and girls playing soccer. They practiced after school on Wednesdays at the Decatur field and had games on Saturday at the YMCA field.

Betty called Dan's house on Saturday morning. "Are you all ready, sweetie? Do you have your little uniform on?" she asked.

"Yes, Mommy," he said.

"Good, I'll be right over. I'll beep for you."

"Okay, I'll look out the window."

It took ten minutes, maybe eleven to get from one house to the other. Betty beeped. Nothing happened. She got out and knocked. No answer. She knocked again. There was no one home, no Dan, no kids, no note, no nothing.

Betty went to the neighbor's house. "Do you know where Dan and the kids are? They were here a few minutes ago. No one mentioned anything about going anywhere. Rhett knew I was on my way over."

"No, I don't know anything," the neighbor said.

Betty had always been a meticulous planner, always on time. She waited a few minutes. Dan knew she was coming and he knew the only reason she was coaching this team was so that their little son could run around and do this stuff.

The whole team was waiting. She had to be there for the other kids. She could feel anger burning like a flame from her belly up. She could almost see Dan's eyes and the look on his face, hard and flat as paint, staring her down and mocking her.

"You son of a bitch," she said, picking up a rock and throwing it through his living-room window.

Next thing she knew she was notified that Dan had gotten a restraining order keeping her one hundred yards away from his house. He failed to mention that it was also her house containing her four kids, all her clothes and furniture, and every possession that she had on earth.

107

Dan started to pull the plug out on seeing the kids. He told the maids and the baby-sitters his wife was crazy. That's why he had the kids. They were not allowed to talk to her or let her come into the house.

Betty was very scared, very nervous. She was still living in temporary quarters with no furniture and no longer allowed to go home or to see her children. She felt horrible.

Christmas came. Dan took the kids and Linda skiing. Betty told her friends she didn't think it was very healthy for the kids to be initiated into the Linda Kolkena situation this way. She said it was not the making of a very memorable family Christmas.

Inside she was teetering on the edge. An image kept returning, an image of her children watching while Dan made love to Linda. Every time she closed her eyes, that image was there.

"Don't worry, Mom," Kim said when she called. They're not sleeping together. There are two beds in the room. "Huh," Betty thought. "A lot she knows." The next day a huge bouquet of flowers arrived from Dan, the biggest she ever received.

"I know you're not feeling well under these difficult circumstances," it said, "but Merry Christmas."

Before the flowers had even died, a letter arrived informing her that Dan was buying another house and he was moving. Betty could pick up her belongings from the garage while he was gone. Otherwise he'd give them to the Salvation Army or throw them away when he returned. He didn't want them anymore.

Dan had finally bought his mansion—a huge classic brick house just like the one his father had. He thought he was getting a real bargain. He didn't understand why no one wanted it. He didn't seem to realize it was a dangerous neighborhood. Now they'd have two new houses, neither one suitable for the kids.

Dan was busy redoing and adding amenities to every inch of his new house, inside and out. He was living like a king. Betty figured he probably spent five hundred thousand dollars just fixing it up, but it still only had three bedrooms. It was so fancy that the children weren't allowed to touch anything.

"I'm not selling the old house," Betty told Ron Jaffe. "It's the only piece of property I've ever owned. The only thing that has my name on it. It's all I have left. I don't care what it's worth on the open market. I don't care what we're offered. My market is closed. No amount of money can force me. A million dollars wouldn't do it." Holding out made Betty feel better. At least she still had control over something.

• 5 •

Janet Baker lived down the street. She and Betty were both lonely and living alone. They both had little dogs and walked them. When Janet walked her dog, she'd put on full jewels and makeup. She'd get ready for two hours just to walk the dog. Betty would be wearing a sweat suit. She wasn't putting on jewelry and five layers of makeup to walk a dog. Janet was always on the lookout, always on show, always using the dog to meet someone. She liked to marry people. She married her last husband when he was seventy-seven years old and she was only thirty. He was her fifth husband. When he died, she inherited trust funds and apartment buildings.

From her boyfriends Janet collected hardware, as she called it—jewels, silver, cars—and when her boyfriends were gone, she would cash it in. That was her life-style. If she saw a better deal at lunchtime, she'd be ready at dinnertime. She was always open to a better deal. It had nothing to do with love or children or affection. It was all a better deal.

She had long blond hair, and when she wasn't walking the dog, she was getting her hair done, getting massages and manicures. She had no children and she was younger than Betty. She and Betty were not really friends, they just lived in the same place.

Janet called one day. She had a friend over who was fixing dinner. He had a friend with him. They needed another woman. Betty was all alone, so she went.

Janet's friend was jumping all over her, hugging and kissing her. All smiles, wearing Connecticut preppy clothes, and looking like he was still in his twenties. Betty thought it was kind of jerky that Janet was with him. "Meet Brad Wright," Janet said. "He dazzles women with his blond, wonderful looks. He's also very rich," she whispered when they were alone. "Born rich, almost Kennedyesque. But he's a playboy. All the women want him."

Betty could see why. He was six feet three inches, blue-eyed, with perfect white teeth, dimples, and a beautiful body. He had been engaged to a young Demi Moore look-alike, Janet said. "But his mother disapproved of her because she wasn't wealthy. After their first meeting his mother sent her an entire box of her old clothes to show her what good taste was. They broke up when she came home from a ski trip and found him with another girl."

Brad's father went to Harvard Business School and then into business. Brad went into business too. Bought a fence company. But it was his mother he was closest to. Brad spoke to his mother every day. Never made a move without her.

After that weekend Brad's nothing-special friend whom Betty had been stuck with went back to San Francisco. But Janet and Brad kept inviting Betty to go out with them as the third wheel, just to be kind.

One night at the yacht club Janet spotted a guy, very tan with a gold chain. She said, "Watch this." She went over to him and began talking, body language and all. Next thing they knew, she'd gone off with him on his boat for three days.

Brad took Betty home. They got together a couple of nights after that. She was supposed to meet him the third night at five o'clock at the dock. They were pals. When Janet came home unexpectedly, Betty said, "You go meet him instead."

Brad called later and said, "Betty, don't ever do that again." It was the first time she ever heard him sound angry. It touched her.

"Janet," Betty said the next day, "if you can tell me that you really like Brad, you can have him. But if you're just using him, I want him."

Betty holding Kim in the early seventies. The picture-perfect image of the happy young mother. COURTESY OF THE BRODERICK FAMILY

Dan and Betty looking into a mirror with Kim in 1968 or 1969, perhaps imagining their perfect future life together. COURTESY OF THE BRODERICK FAMILY

Dan and Betty discovering the coastline of La Jolla, the jewel that would become their new home. COURTESY OF THE BRODERICK FAMILY

This was the moment Betty had been waiting for: The Brodericks finally had their dream house in La Jolla, the children were happy and healthy, and her husband was financially successful. Little did she know that Dan was just about to embark on his affair with Linda. COURTESY OF THE BRODERICK FAMILY

Danny hugs his mother on a sailing trip in happier times. COURTESY OF THE BRODERICK FAMILY

1983: This photograph of the Broderick children was probably taken the "first Christmas of my devastation," as Betty referred to that first Christmas after discovering the affair between her husband and Linda Kolkena. From top left, clockwise: Lee, Kim, Rhett, and Danny. COURTESY OF THE BRODERICK FAMILY

Betty and Dan at a 1983 dinner dance celebrating the works of Re Boudreau, a San Diego lawyer. He had just begun his affair with Linda. COURTESY OF SPENCER BUSBY

A portrait of Betty in 1986, which shows the strain and tension left on Betty's face after an emotionally and physically draining year. COURTESY OF THE BRODERICK FAMILY

Linda and Dan at the Red
Boudreau dinner dance in 1987.

Growing exasperated with her lawyers, Betty decided to serve as her
own attorney in order to get a custody and financial settlement just
before Dan's marriage to Linda in
1989.

Betty, looking dazed and exhausted after days of arguing over custody and property with the judge. She has lost her voice and come down with the flu.
COPYRIGHT © JOE KLEIN

Dan and Linda's colonial house the morning the murders took place. The white car parked in front belonged to Dan and Linda. COURTESY OF SPENCER BUSBY

Betty's first court appearance after the murders, on her forty-third birthday.
COPYRIGHT © ROBERT BURROUGHS

"I'm just using him," Janet admitted.

Brad liked having Betty as his date. Even though she had gained some weight, she was beautiful in the same elegant way that his mother was beautiful. The young girls he usually brought home with junior dresses and mod hairstyles always made his mother say, "Where'd you find her?" But not Betty. Brad's mother loved Betty. Betty was older than Brad by seven years. She knew how to dress. She was committed to her own family and not trying to marry this gorgeous young son of hers.

Betty and Brad both made it clear that they would stay just pals. He always had lots of girls. He thought of Betty almost as his mother, and she thought of him almost as one of her adorable, pesky little boys. That was what each of them missed most.

She didn't want to be like Dan, the other half of the middle-aged joke.

She felt uncomfortable, not flattered by the age difference. He took her to black-tie affairs, but she never took him anywhere as her date. She didn't want to give people anything to talk about. She didn't want to count on him and never felt she could. She thought he might meet some young girl at any time and never be back.

Betty also wasn't ready for anything but a friendship.

Just the same, Brad would stop by to eat, or watch television. Sometimes he'd spend the night in one of the empty kid's rooms. She'd call him her puppy dog—very playful and so cute. But when her real kids were around, she'd ignore him.

Sometimes she'd go to football weekends with him and his friends and their dates. They were all young girls. She didn't fit in. It wasn't even that she looked so different. It was more that she had four kids and that she was still married to Dan in her heart. These girls were just starting out.

Betty was somewhere between Brad's still-glamorous and beautiful mother in her sixties and these girls in their twenties or early thirties. She didn't belong in either place. Still, it was fun having Brad come around in his little shorts and striped sailor shirts. It didn't mean that much, she told herself. But it helped her climb out of the misery, at least for short periods of time.

111

Betty was afraid to make love. Brad had so many women lovers. He never wanted any commitment or any responsibility. If a girl he dated wanted to marry him, he was gone. If a man came on to Betty, she'd run like a scared rabbit.

They were parallel, not together. He was not saying, "Marry me," or "I love you," and she was not saying, "Where were you at eight o'clock on Friday night?" He was very nice to her, but he never ever said he loved her. She never said, "Why did you look at that other girl?" There was none of that romantic tension, none of that insecurity. He was wonderful, but she couldn't see herself being with him any more than with Brian. She couldn't actually see herself being with anyone except Dan and her children.

• 6 •

"Hi, this is the Broderick residence. We're out and about. Leave a message and we'll call you back." The voice on the answering machine was clipped, girlish, almost childlike. There was a tight, pressured quality that Betty couldn't quite identify. It was her children's private line, but the voice was Linda Kolkena's.

Betty felt a shock come through those wires and enter her body.

Images sprang up like ghosts. Her life was going on without her.

They were all together. Like a family. This girl was replacing her. Everything was going on as usual, except that she had been locked out of her own family. It felt as if she was being dropped like a stone into a well.

"You whore, you cunt," she said out loud. "You've stolen my husband. You've stolen my children, you've stolen my house, you've stolen my life." She picked up the phone and dialed again. She couldn't hear that message enough, and she couldn't believe she was hearing it. Where were her children now?. Where was Dan, her husband, her love, the prince of her girlhood dreams?

112

"Can't you stop fucking the cunt long enough to come to the phone?" she yelled into the machine, hardly recognizing her own voice. She dialed again. "Stop screwing the cunt long enough to return my calls. I have very important things to ask you." Betty kicked the wall, then pounded it with her fists. "You're making me mad. I'll kill you."

It was as if a dam had broken and all the repressed rage had come crashing through. There were no controls on anything now. The primitive force had taken over, wilder and more savage after all the years of passive acceptance, all the years of building.

Betty hung up. Her eyes burned with tears. She wiped them away with her skirt and picked up the phone again. Even the dial tone stung. Linda's message came on, but it was Dan she was thinking of. "I'm having so much fun," Betty said. "I love this machine? I want to go to court to prove you're a fuckhead and she's a cunt, and I'll win. I love it. This is going to be so much fun. Ha-ha, cunt. What are you doing on the machine? Don't you have a toilet of your own to live in?"

Betty took a deep breath. All of a sudden the room was turning black. She strained against the darkness and dialed again.

"Fuckhead," she said. "You've made my life a nightmare. I can't go to sleep. I close my eyes and see you and the cunt doing it. Doing all your wonderful things." The words hurt. She thought she had lost her voice. The pounding pain in her head was back.

"And, ummm," she said, as her voice cracked, "you're going to be real sorry."

• 7 •

Next thing she knew, Dan left for a three-week first-class European vacation with Linda. While he was gone, Marika, the new baby-sitter called. "I'm not supposed to call you. But I don't know what to do," Marika said. "This is only Wednesday of the first week, and we have

113

no more money. We need food. Lee is sick. She needs medicine. Mr. Broderick gave me three checks for a hundred dollars, each postdated so we could only use one a week. We can't wait until next Monday."

"Four kids on a hundred dollars a week," Betty said. "That's even less than he's been giving me. What a guy. I bet he's spending more than that an hour on the cunt. I'll be right over."

"But you're not allowed," Marika said. "There's a restraining order against you."

"What the hell am I supposed to do, let my kids starve?" Betty answered. "Besides, it's reached a point where breaking Dan's rules is one of my few remaining pleasures."

Betty emptied her medicine cabinet and refrigerator, then she stopped at the supermarket and bought another hundred dollars' worth of groceries. She also cashed a check for one hundred dollars.

Marika was very nice, but she was nervous. Dan had told her that if she saw Betty, she should call the police immediately. It didn't take her long to make her own judgments. After that they had a great time together.

"It's like night and day," Marika said. "When Mr. Broderick is here, the children are so tense." Betty made a few of her specialties and was over there two to three times while Dan was gone. She had a ball. Marika and the kids did too.

Shortly after Dan got back, a letter arrived to punish her for coming to his house while he was away and for the obscene phone calls on his answering machine. He was establishing a system of fines.

Every time she called Linda a name, it was going to cost her five hundred dollars. Every time she came within a hundred yards of his house, it was going to cost her a thousand dollars. Every time she came into his house, it would cost her five thousand dollars. The fines were retroactive. Betty's monthly allowance for November 1985, after he added up all her fines from October, was minus thirteen hundred dollars.

"Very funny, Dan," she said out loud, and then she began to shake. Betty knew she had to fight back. Dan still hadn't paid Ron Jaffe, so she figured he wouldn't help. She got all dressed up. At about four-thirty she called Dian Black. "I'm going over there to talk to him about these fines," she said. I'm bringing my purse phone. If he tries anything, I'll call you. If he arrests me, call Brad."

Dan was in the front yard gardening.

"Dan," she said, starting off calmly, "what am I supposed to do with minus thirteen hundred dollars?"

"If you don't leave my property in the next ten seconds," he answered without looking up at her, "I'll have you arrested."

"That's okay," Betty answered. "I'll just keep coming back until we settle this thing. The new house, my car, everything I have except the old house is in your name. If you don't give me any money, I'll lose the house I'm living in. I won't have anywhere to go anyhow."

Dan walked toward his house. "I'm going out tonight," he said. "I've got to get dressed." He went inside and closed the door.

"I think he's calling the cops," Betty whispered to Dian on the cellular phone. "But I'm not moving."

"There's a restraining order against you, ma'am," the police officer said when he arrived a few minutes later. "You have to leave. If you don't, I'll arrest you."

"Officer," she said, "I have nowhere to go and no money. I'm not leaving until we work this out. It costs me six thousand dollars to pay my bills before I even spend anything. I'm trapped and I'm desperate."

He snapped handcuffs on her and put her into the backseat. As he pulled away from the curb, Betty turned around from the rear window of the police car. She saw Dan and Linda coming out of the house. Dan was wearing his tuxedo, his cape, and his top hat. They were leaving for the Blackstone Ball. He was officially about to be named president of the San Diego Bar Association.

It was Betty's first time in the Las Calinas Prison. The cinderblock structure with the small barred waiting room and the holding tank beyond it was less than an hour from La Jolla, but it seemed like the other end of the earth. She was fingerprinted, her mug shot was taken, then she was stripped and searched. To this day Betty can't remember any of it, not going there or how long she stayed or the what the cell was like, or even when Brad finally picked her up and took her home.

One thing she did remember, though, was that a few days later an envelope arrived in the mail. Inside was a photograph of Dan and Linda laughing. It was taken at the Blackstone Ball. There was a note attached. She thought it was from Linda. The note said, "It must kill you to see these two happy together. Eat your heart out, bitch."

• 8 •

Betty's parents came. The boys were finally visiting. Betty had cooked a pork roast. The house was still empty but now it seemed almost festive. They were just getting ready to sit down to dinner at a make-shift table when the phone rang.

"Betty," Ron Jaffe said. "Dan sold your house in court today. He got a special dispensation from the judge called a four-hour notice. In theory you had four hours to object; in fact you didn't know about it."

"That's impossible. He couldn't. My name is on that deed."

"It's almost impossible," Jaffe said, correcting her. "But he managed."

Betty knew she had infuriated Dan when she refused to accept an offer on the house. But that was her house. She loved it. Her heart and soul of a house. The only house they'd ever had.

Betty also knew that Jaffe still hadn't received the ten-thousand-dollar retainer from Dan. Even if the special order from the judge allowing Dan to sell was legal, there was no way that notifying only Jaffe and not Betty could be. He wasn't her official attorney. She didn't have one.

"They got away with that," she gasped. "You're not even my lawyer. Isn't that the point of having your name on property, so one person can't decide when and how much they're going to sell it for behind your back and keep your half?" Her heart was racing. "That's the man

116

I've been married to for twenty years. Does he remember me? Does he remember that twenty years ago he married me?"

"We can expect this kind of thing thoughout the whole proceeding," Jaffe answered.

"Then why in the name of God did you let me think that you could help? When you're going through a divorce, you do a chalkboard, Dan's things and my things. That's all I had on my side of the chalkboard. The only thing that had my name on it was half of that house. He just disposed of it right away, just like that. The son of a bitch got a special judge's order. That leaves my bargaining power at absolutely nothing." She was shaking. "Nothing else on earth has my name on it, nothing. I stupidly thought Dan could cheat me out of everything else, but he couldn't cheat me out of our house. Thanks, Mr. Jaffe, I've gotta go."

"I'll be right back," Betty said to her parents. "I have to talk to Dan."

She drove blindly. She was looking at the road but seeing her life pass before her. She remembered meeting Dan, marrying him, having Kim, finding that house, buying it, fixing it up. There were a lot more memories, but they were so far inside her and they hurt so much. She didn't know if she really wanted to recall them.

Dan's life was completely on schedule. He was traveling. He was working. He had his full-time, live-in girlfriend. He had his four children. He had all the assets and all the income. She had nothing. Even the house she was living in now was in his name. The leased car that had no equity was in his name. He had canceled all the credit cards. She had no money of her own, nothing, none, zero.

He would not retain Mr. Jaffe because Mr. Jaffe was a good lawyer. Except for a couple of friendly guys that she couldn't really connect with, her life had come to a screeching halt. She couldn't go left, she couldn't go right, she couldn't go forward or backward.

Betty jammed on the brakes wondering what she should do. She felt trapped, cornered, overpowered, bullied, like she was being sat on and tied and bound and gagged. She was fighting and struggling, but she was losing.

Dan wasn't home from work yet. Betty waited with Kim and Lee.

Kim snuck away and called her father. "Dad, come home, hurry," she said. "Mom's here and she's really mad that you sold the house."

"Call the police," Dan said. Kim hung up, confused. She didn't want to get her mother in trouble. Besides, what was she supposed to say to the police—"My mom came over"? That sounded dumb. She went back to Betty. "Mom, you're not allowed to be here," Kim said. Then she started crying.

When Dan pulled up, his face was gray. "You have ten seconds to get off my property," he said. Then he started counting. "Ten, nine, eight, seven, six . . ."

"Girls," Betty said, "be my witnesses. I just want to ask him what he did with my house."

"Talk to your lawyer," Dan snapped.

"The same lawyer you refused to send a retainer to. You know he'll do nothing for me." The pitch of Betty's voice rose. "What did you do with my house? Dan, who did you sell it to? How much did you get? What about my half? I own half, you know. The law says I own half."

"The law says you own half," Dan answered. "But it doesn't say I have to give it to you." He walked past her into the house.

Betty turned and jumped into her car. She drove crazily. She needed Dan. She needed to talk to him. She didn't know who Dan was anymore. She needed the old Dan.

Then she was angry again, feeling like she'd rather destroy the house than have him steal it from her. She ran into a gas station and bought a gallon of gasoline. She backed up, pulled out, and took off. Then she drove back over to the house. Half of it was hers. She loved the house. Betty poured gasoline on the stairs and lit a match. The edges of the carpet seared, smoked, and went out.

The kids had been so happy and so safe here. They had had each other and their own rooms, and she had them. She didn't want to destory this house. This wasn't what she wanted to do. She wanted Dan, she wanted her husband. She wanted her life back.

Betty got back in the car again and began racing back toward Dan's. Nothing was clear. She loved him. She hated him. She needed him. She couldn't reach him. She saw his house. She was right there in front getting ready to step on the brake. "Fuck you," she said out loud. "Pow on you. How dare you. How dare you do this to me and the kids." She lifted her foot off the brake and put it back on the gas. The car plowed into Dan's front door.

Dan and the girls were in the kitchen making dinner. They heard the noise. It kept going, it sounded like a chain saw. Kim screamed and ran out the back door, through the backyard and down into the canyon beyond it. As she ran, she could hear Dan yelling. Finally the noise stopped. Kim hid in the bushes crying.

"What the hell are you doing," Dan yelled. "What the fuck do you think you're doing?" She had gotten out of the car. She was hitting him on the head with her keys. He had her by the shoulders. They were wrestling. Lee got in the middle, trying to stop them. They were squashing her. Dan was trying to get Lee out of the way. He pushed her aside and punched Betty in the chest. She fell on the ground.

Kim could hear the police sirens from all the way down in the canyon. She crept out and walked back up the hill crying. Kim couldn't help it. She cried a lot. When she got near the front of the house, she saw the police putting her mother in a straitjacket. She watched them force her into the back of the police car and take her away.

• 9 •

Betty had never been in a loony bin before. She had a book on Thomas Jefferson in her purse. She was too upset to talk, so she sat in the waiting room where everybody was going nuts, reading *Thomas Jefferson, Volume II.*

Finally they took her into a little room and gave her an interview. "Do you have a drug problem? Do you have a drinking problem? Are you hallucinating? Are you hearing voices?" the guy asked.

"No," Betty told them. "The only problem I really have in the whole world right now is I can't get a lawyer who will defend me against my husband. I don't really have any problems that a good lawyer couldn't take care of for me."

The intake officer looked at her as if she was crazy. The doctor Dan had called the last time he tried to get her committed came into the room. He wanted to examine her. Betty refused. She wouldn't deal with him. Finally they brought in a consultant. He told her to commit herself. "No, thank you," she said. "I'd rather not."

"As soon as the seventy-two-hour hold is up, I'm out of here. I'm not crazy. I'm pissed off. The man has given me every good reason to be. It's not like I drove through town and for no reason took a right through his front door. And I didn't drive through his house. I didn't go into the picture window in the front and out the back of the house into the swimming pool. I bumped into his fucking door on purpose, to say, 'Fuck you,' because he had just said, 'Fuck you' to me, and I didn't like it. I did it because you can't just let someone do that to you and not protest in some way."

They led her to her sleeping quarters. She was cold. There were no sheets, no blankets, no nothing in the room.

The next morning while walking past the front desk Betty heard one of the aides, a skinny kid with pimples, whisper, "She slept in her clothes all night. I'm going to write it down." Betty turned and walked up to the desk and said, "Not only did I sleep in my clothes, but I was so cold that I got up and put my shoes on. I didn't have anything else. You didn't give me anything else, not even a sheet or a blanket. What would you expect me to sleep in?"

The aide stared at her wordlessly. "She's demented, she's wacko," the aide whispered as Betty walked away.

While she was in the loony bin, Betty called Charles Jacobson, a child psychiatrist who was also a friend. Dr. Jacobson was sick in bed himself. He made many phone calls trying to get her an attorney, then told her he was astonished by the response and had never experienced anything like it.

"I told you," Betty said. "Did you think I was lying?"

"No," he answered. "I didn't think you were lying, but I didn't think you had tried hard enough."

120

• 10 •

In July she got another four-hour notice. She still had no lawyer. Dan had never paid Jaffe the retainer. She called the courtroom.

"Look," she said to the clerk. "I just got this four-hour notice. My husband is going to court for some kind of divorce proceeding and I can't get an attorney. I have appointments with attorneys all week. I have an appointment tomorrow. Can we put this off until I get an attorney?"

"No," the clerk said.

This was 1986. Dan's framed portrait was on the wall of the courthouse, a big, handsome picture. Everytime Betty walked past it, she wanted to put gum on his nose. Only one thing stopped her. She figured he would put her in jail for that too.

"It doesn't matter that your husband is the president of the bar association. There are five thousand lawyers in this town. I'm sure you can find one," the clerk said. He hung up.

How could she go into that courtroom alone and defend herself against Dan Broderick, Harvard-educated litigator and president of the bar? Dan Broderick and his expert legal counsel. She was scared to death. Whenever Dan wanted a delay, he got one with no problem. Betty figured if she wasn't there, the judge would be forced to postpone it. Wrong. At that ex parte hearing, Dan divorced Betty. The final divorce decree gave her no court-ordered community property, no monthly support, no custody, and no visitation rights to any of her four children. The judge agreed that all of these issues would be settled at an unspecified later date. Meanwhile Dan and Betty were divorced. He called this bifurcation. Betty called it bifornication, a way legally to fuck your wife and girlfriend at the same time.

Brad's family was really trying to help. Brad had an uncle, a lovely gray-haired attorney. The uncle was not a divorce attorney, but he felt terrible when he heard what was happening. He knew Dan Broderick. He felt so bad that he got a young lawyer to come over to his office the next day and meet Betty.

121

She was trying to hold her head up, but she still couldn't stop crying. She could not get out of her car to get into the building to walk to the elevator to go to the office. She was late. She knew she was supposed to be up there, but she could barely even breathe. She had her dignity here. She was trying to pretend that she was okay.

Finally she did it. She told him the whole thing as well as she could. Here was this young associate, he had no secretary, he was just starting out. He looked discouraged and completely overwhelmed. "We may go down," he said, "but we'll go down fighting."

Oh, shit, Betty thought. This young man might have good intentions, but Dan Broderick would do the fandango on his face. It would just be a joke if this kid in polyester pants went into court against Dan Harvard Broderick. So she said, "Thank you, thank you very much, I appreciate your concern, but you're not the kind of lawyer I need. The kind of lawyer I need very rarely goes into divorce. There are very few of them. Ron Jaffe was one, and the other ones that I called were all Dan's friends."

Betty went home and started scouting the newspapers. There was an ad in the paper about a divorce mediator. She called. The next day she went and met him. He agreed to mediate the divorce.

Dan came to one appointment. He walked in with a yellow jacket and a plaid tie and a yellow flower in his lapel, the hottest peacock that ever walked. He sat there and he said, "First this, and second that, and third this, and fourth that." He wasn't in there for five minutes and he got up and left. The lawyer turned to Betty. "Obviously, this isn't going to work," he said. Betty nodded. It was very clear that Dan Broderick wasn't going to submit to mediation. But he said, "I'm a lawyer and I will take your case."

"Thank you very very much," Betty said. "You're a real sweet guy. You've got nice blue eyes, but Dan Broderick will chew you up and spit you out. You are a mediator. You are a 'let's get together, let's make a deal, let's be friendly' kind of guy. Dan Broderick is a go-for-the-jugular, killer trial lawyer. He has no mercy. He kills the other side. The more he kills, the more he wins. He has no kindness, not one vein in his body. You are on the opposite end of the spectrum of how lawyers do things. Thank you very much, but no thank you."

The lawyer wrote to Dan's lawyer anyhow and said he'd take the case. Dan jumped at it and sent him ten thousand dollars of Betty's community share without checking with her. The same ten thousand dollars he would never send Jaffe. He did it, Betty figured, because he thought this guy couldn't win.

The new lawyer was supposed to finalize plans to get Betty the kids for Christmas. She was going to take them skiing—Dan had promised to send money. She made reservations. The whole thing was set. Then Dan reneged. Not only didn't she get to take the kids skiing, she was barred from seeing them over the entire holiday.

On Christmas morning Betty called her parents. "Merry Christmas," she said. She was lying on her bed. She could hardly get the words out. "What's wrong, honey?" her father asked. Betty began to cry. The whole story poured out. "I want my kids. Daddy, I miss my kids."

"Yeah," her dad said, sounding a little frightened, "but besides that, everything's okay?"

" 'Besides that,' Daddy? Don't you understand? There is no 'besides that.' That's it. That's my whole world."

Brad had come into the house. He was standing at the door to the bedroom, listening. He walked over to the bed and lay down. "Come with me tonight," he said gently. "Don't stay here alone. Come out to dinner."

Normally Betty would have loved the black-tie banquet Brad was going to. "No," she said. "It's Christmas. I have to stay here in case they call. I have to be here for them. It's important to me that my kids know I'm here."

He took Betty in his arms and held her while she cried. He kissed her and sheltered her, and for the first time he made love to her.

It was a giant step. Before this he'd lie on the bed and watch TV and fall asleep and she'd get up and go to bed in the other room. They'd play cat and mouse. Never, never before had she experienced anything like this from a man.

She was forty years old and it was her first real experience with tenderness.

• 11 •

Betty Broderick on Brad and Dan

"When Brad asked me one night what movie I wanted to go to, I said, 'Do you realize that no one has ever asked me what movie I wanted to go to before? No one has ever asked me. If Dan wanted to go to a movie, he was like, "We're going to a movie. If you go get a baby-sitter, you can come. If you can't get a baby-sitter, I'm going without you." He never said, "What type of movie would you like to go to, honey? What restaurant would you like to go to? What would you like to do?" Never once in his life did he say, "What would you like to do?" '

"With Brad, in some ways, it was just the opposite. It was always so much fun with him. We'd go down to the beach and he'd have his arm around me, or I'd have my arm around him or something. Dan and I never did anything physical like that. He was much more proper, because that's the way we were raised and that's how our marriage was. There was not a whole bunch of physical romance, because we were married and he didn't have to do all that.

"Brad wasn't courting me, either, in the traditional sense. Brad gave me one present in three years. The third Christmas he gave me a frying pan, and I have never cooked with it because I'm saving it to hit him over the head with. I cooked for him all the time. This is a lovely frying pan. It's from some gourmet shop, but I have about twelve frying pans. He has never given me even a dandelion. He has never given me anything, nothing. That wasn't our relationship.

"One night Brad did tell me I looked gorgeous. I went out with Brad to a New Year's Eve party. They had the picture at the trial, black and white. I had this real pretty dress on. Brad walked me to the kitchen of my house, and I turned around, and he just went, 'Oh, my

God, you look gorgeous.' But he never said, 'I love you.'" He took me to all kinds of weddings and parties and things, and I had a wonderful time. But I was with him in name only.

"In my mind I was still married to Dan. He was divorced from me, but I was married. I was economically married in the sense that I had absolutely nothing that I owned independently from him, no roof over my head, no car, no food, no savings, no nothing that I could feel secure about.

"I was also still married emotionally. I married Dan in the true sense of the word, that two shall become one. I was married for so long that when we split up, it was like part of me died or was still part of him. Yes, I had my disappointments, like being raped on our wedding night, but they were never enough to make me stop loving him. I always wrote everything off until Linda.

"We were raised that way, Dan and I, to be a couple, forever."

• 12 •

The mediator had gone skiing himself—probably, Betty figured, with the ten thousand dollars of her community property. As far as she could see, he hadn't prepared for the December 30th hearing. He never requested receipts from Dan to substantiate their former life-style. He went to court with what he called family-law guidelines, which no one else had ever heard of. In calculating Betty's expenses he forgot to include income tax, medical and home insurance, house taxes, car payments, and club dues.

He settled on nine thousand dollars a month, the same amount Betty was getting from Dan back in 1985 when he was still paying the other bills.

"Yes," Betty said. "I know it sounds like a lot of money, but Dan is making more than one hundred thousand dollars a month. The mortgage payments and house bill alone are over six thousand dollars. If I keep up the life-style that we are used to, I'll be seven thousand dollars in the hole each month. Frankly I don't see why I shouldn't keep that life-style. I spent twenty years building up to it with Dan. He's keeping it. After what I've been through, he owes it to me."

Betty began calling San Diego lawyers again. She wanted someone who would really fight back. They all turned her down. Finally she found another lawyer in Los Angeles who said he would take the case. He also wanted a ten-thousand-dollar retainer before getting started.

"I don't have it," she said.

"I'm not surprised," he answered, chuckling and eyeing her gold and diamond necklace. "I'll take that as a retainer instead of money." Betty took off the necklace and handed it to him.

"Jaffe still wants five thousand dollars for his services," she told Brad that night. "The mediator says I owe him two or three thousand more. The newest lawyer took my necklace, and I still have nothing to show for it."

• 13 •

She felt battered, not physically but more continually than a person who gets punched or pushed down every once in a while. It was a constant control battle. Now they were divorced, but he still had control over her house, her car, her money, her children. As she saw it, he could throw her in jail or take away anything from her anytime he wanted, just like that. She felt like a frightened, miniature person, completely at his mercy, and he'd proved over and over that he had none.

"It's him or me," she told Brad. "I'm in a corner here with my children huddled against me and nowhere to turn. I've lost it all. I don't know anyone else who has. Even if a plane goes down, people don't usually lose all their children and their husband. And if they do, they still have their home, their in-laws, and their extended family on their side. I don't even have that backing. Dan's family has nothing against me, but since this came along, I've never heard from them. They didn't know what to say or what to do. So they didn't do anything. My own family won't have anything to do with it. Divorce is something that they just don't do. If they ignore it, they think it will just go away."

"Come on, Betty," Brad said, trying to change the subject. "Let's go down to the club. Let's go sailing."

"Don't you understand, Brad, I can't forget about this. I'm Betty Broderick, Dan's wife, the kids' mother, the woman who lived in the house Dan sold. The woman who made that house. I'm just torn from all my moorings, just bobbing around out there in the sea. I can't do anything. I have no direction at all. I'm searching for one. But if I can't get my children stabilized and happy, I don't have the energy to do anything else. They're my number-one priority, and I have so much guilt about not being able to take care of them."

Betty slumped down on the couch. She couldn't shake it. In 1986 she was upset about the divorce, but she still thought that someday it would be over. She thought from that moment forward she would build a new life. Now she had lost all hope of ever getting anything, her children, her house, justice in any court. She had no energy to stay awake and she couldn't sleep.

Betty was capable of taking care of those children and she wanted to do that more than anything in the world. Even when she and Dan were young and poor, she prided herself on doing a beautiful job. Her kids always had high self-esteem and they always looked just perfect. Even before they had a dime in the bank, Kim had a little gold bangle bracelet that was engraved with her name from Saks.

Betty made things by hand then, matching little dresses from remnants that cost eighty-nine cents a yard for the fabric. She still had pictures of the girls in those dresses. They were always well mannered, neat, clean, with the best food, and at the top of their class, all four of them. She couldn't bear to stand by and watch it all go to hell.

Rhett called in the middle of the night. He had an earache. He was afraid to go to Daddy's door. Daddy was in bed with Linda. "Daddy might not even answer. Or he might yell." Rhett wanted a hug and a kiss. He wanted to climb into bed next to his mommy so that she could take care of him. But Mommy wasn't there because Daddy had sole custody with no visitation.

When Dan wasn't around, they called her ten, twenty times a day. Dan found out. Next thing Betty knew, the phones were locked in the closet so that the kids couldn't call her. Worse, the ringers were turned off so that they couldn't hear her calling them. Sometimes they'd sneak out to a phone and call, crying, saying they'd been waiting all day for her to call them. Betty would call them back and the machine with Linda's voice would come on again. It drove her wild.

"Rhetty-pooh, it's your mama. It's nine-thirty at night and I just got home and got the message that you need to know something. . . . I'll call back a couple of times, maybe you'll hear it ring."

"Rhetty-pooh, it's your mom. It's the morning. What do you need to know, honey? I'll just keep calling back and hoping you hear the ringer. You called last night. You need to know something. What do you need to know? It's almost time for you to get on the bus." Still no answer. She was infuriated. She lost all judgment and all restraint.

"Has the cunt been playing with the phone again?" she yelled, feeling the pressure inside her burst out.

Betty felt trapped. If she tried to confront Dan in person, she'd go to jail. If she tried to call him, he wouldn't take her phone calls. He wouldn't speak to her. She kept calling and getting the machine. She felt angry and helpless. She dialed again. "Hey, fuckhead," she said. "You really picked the wrong person to fight with. I will parade every person in San Diego County you ever met to testify loudly what a drunken, selfish, coldhearted, rotten bastard you were every year of your life to your wife and your kids. All this mess with Linda and everyone else. You're going to be so sorry you started this, you stupid ass."

Even as she did it, Betty could hear herself damaging her own chances. But she couldn't stop. Her rage had a voice of its own.

129

Dan took her back to court for those phone calls. At least she had replaced the L.A. lawyer who wanted her jewelry with Tricia Smith, a tall, thin, elegant Del Mar lawyer whom she liked a lot. On the way into court Tricia presented Betty with a fifteen-thousand-dollar IOU payable on demand. Betty was shocked, but she had no choice. She needed someone to defend her, so she signed.

"Ah, Mr. Broderick," the judge said, smiling, as Dan entered the courtroom. "To what do we owe this honor?" Betty knew she was dead meat. Tricia did a great job. She pointed out that the phone was the only means of communication Betty had left with her kids. There were no restraining orders on that. She pointed out that the kids missed Betty very much and called every day crying and leaving messages that said, "Call me back."

They played a tape from Danny saying he was running away from Daddy's house because he'd rather live nowhere than live there if he couldn't see Mommy. The judge nodded, said, "Get the girlfriend off the machine," then sentenced Betty to twenty-eight days in jail. "Can't she at least go home and lock up her house?" Tricia pleaded. The request was denied. Betty was handcuffed and carted off to prison.

"Don't feel bad, Tricia. You did a great job," Betty said before they took her. "We're just not playing with a full deck here against the president of the bar. You saw it. The judge was awed by his presence in a courtroom. You know something, I don't care what they do to me. I'll never stop communicating with my kids. They love me and they need me—now more than ever."

• 14 •

Betty made the rounds of organizations for abused women. The members of HALT (Help Abolish Legal Abuse) were outraged by her treatment. Ronnie Brown and Dian Black became her friends. Some-times when their kindness made her drop the angry façade, she'd break down and cry. Betty was tired. She gave the diary she had been keeping for three years to Dian. She figured that way in case she killed herself, her kids could read it and find out what had really happened.

Dan Broderick was grossing more than $110,000 a month. Under the mediator's temporary court order, he was still giving her $9,000. Based on that she was able to get credit cards again. He claimed to net $67,000 and said his living costs were $33,000 a month. Betty could also play that game. She went out and bought everything in sight, saved all the receipts, and put her own monthly living costs at $27,000. Her legal bills were $500,000. It worked. The judge granted Betty temporary support of $16,000 a month. She was finally seeing the boys on alternate weekends.

PART V

• • •

Over
the Edge

"I used to joke around in school that the worst thing that could happen to me would be for me to finish medical school, law school, pass the bar, and then be killed. If I were told I had a short time left to live, I'd be shattered. I'd feel I had wasted my whole life."

—*Excerpt from a letter Dan wrote to Betty on November 5, 1976, exactly thirteen years before he was killed*

• 1 •

The wedding was set for April, on the closest Saturday to Dan and Betty's twenty-year anniversary. Betty read about it in the newspaper. She was standing outside her own life, watching it being replayed without her. She wanted to know every detail.

Delivering the boys back to Dan's, Betty picked up an envelope lying on his front porch. She was feeling pretty detached. She had no idea, no thought in her head about a wedding list. "Looky here, isn't this interesting," she said to the children as she opened the envelope. "He's inviting the tax accountant, the one who valued everything for him, and the child psychiatrist who never met me but said you guys should stay with him. And here are the judges who ruled against me. Looks more like a thank-you-for-helping-me-screw-my-wife party than a wedding-invitation list."

Betty didn't want to get caught standing there, so she stuck it in her purse. It was just a scratch-paper thing that he'd left out for the engraver. It didn't hold up his plans for a minute, but Dan made a humongous big deal out of it.

He called Betty into court and canceled the sixteen thousand dollars. "If he wanted the list, all he had to do was say so," she said. "I would have said, 'Here's your stupid list.' Instead he dragged me into court and made me sign all kinds of papers promising I wouldn't contact anyone on the list, even my own longtime relatives and friends. He's pretending I'm calling everyone in town telling them not to attend his stupid wedding. I couldn't be bothered. Please."

The court ordered the kids to be at Dan's wedding the following April. Highly improper, Betty thought, because the kids were very undecided about going to the wedding. "Look, the kids could stay at my house that weekend," Betty said to the judge. "If they want to go to the wedding, I will do nothing to stop them. I will even drive them over, but I think they should be given the choice. They should not be ordered to stay over there. I think it's very sad for the children."

"I'm sorry," the judge answered. He wouldn't change it.

• 2 •

Some mornings Betty would wake up early and start flipping through the catalogs. She could be ordering from the East Coast three hours before the San Diego stores were even open. It wasn't that she needed anything. Figuring out what to order took her mind off the wedding the way walking on the beach helped her to get air in her lungs. It allowed her to slip away a little and reduce some of the pressure building up inside her head.

She'd be the first to say she already had a closetful of grotesquely expensive clothes, all bought on credit. A $40,000 fur coat, two fur jackets, a couple of gowns at $8,000 each, and some everyday outfits that cost about $2,000 apiece. She hardly ever wore the clothes, preferring sweat suits. It all just hung in her closet with the tags still on. She offered the clothes to her friends. She always kept her closet open.

Helen Picard liked Betty's things and took her up on it more than once. She liked Betty's style, her class, her intelligence. Helen thought Betty could do almost anything. They'd known each other nearly fourteen years. Their kids were practically the same age. Helen was one of the La Jolla mothers who had dropped her baby off at Betty's for day care. At one point they owned a piece of property together along with their husbands. For a couple of years Helen had been going through a divorce of her own and didn't see Betty much, but in the last year or two they'd become closer again.

Even now Helen thought Betty had it all. When her settlement left her with three kids and only three hundred dollars a month in support, Helen started a janitorial service. She made the contacts to clean buildings for La Jolla cocktail parties, then contracted the work out.

Helen had always been independent and resourceful. Her own father had been killed in Japan when she was only six. As the oldest child it had fallen on her to help her mother, who never remarried. She was a war orphan who had gotten government help with her education.

After graduating from Mount Saint Mary's College in L.A., she married and supported her husband through college. She had one child at twenty-three and the next one five years later. Five years after that she ended up adopting a little boy; one of the local nuns had called and asked her to take the baby for a while. He was a hard baby to place because his health was poor. Helen felt connected to orphans. After all, she knew what it was like to lose a parent.

When it came to losing a husband, Helen was confused. She had divorced hers. Ended it by free choice. Why Betty didn't just get on with her life was beyond Helen. Sixteen thousand dollars a month sounded like a million. Helen thought money was the issue, and hatred was the problem, because that's what Betty talked about. She believed that people said what they meant, not the opposite.

"You want to get revenge, lose weight," Helen suggested. "Become a lawyer. Do something really good. Show him how smart you are." She might as well have been talking to a wall.

Betty was in a different world. She couldn't let go. The boundaries between her and Dan had merged. Outside she was shouting, "I hate the fucker. Sixteen thousand isn't enough." Inside she was crying, *We're one and the same forever. Such a perfect family. We had it all. We even had money. We made it, Dan. We finally made it.*

Betty went to the courtroom in her jogging suit. Maybe it was self-destructive not to get all dressed up like Dan did, but she had given up. She couldn't be a lawyer. She couldn't compete. She was a housewife. No, worse, she was a throwaway housewife. But even a throwaway housewife had some rights. She sat down in the back row and waited all day. When he was done with his full calender, Judge Murphy looked up at her. After all these years he knew who she was. "What do you want?" he asked.

"I want a court date. I want a courtroom. I want my money," she answered. "It's been five years. Dan's getting married in April. I still have no divorce settlement. I haven't even been able to get a good lawyer. I've wasted a hundred thousand dollars and I have nothing to show for it. I'm not getting a lawyer now. I'll represent myself. I can't lose any more than I've already lost and I can do it for free. I want a settlement."

Betty was looking directly into his eyes. "You can arrest me and put me back in jail, but I'm not going home until you give me a court date. If you arrest me and put me in jail, I'm coming back as soon as I get out. If you arrest me again, I'm coming back again, because I'm not dying for you people."

The judge looked down. He opened his book. "December twenty-sixth," he said. It would be her third Christmas in a row in court, in a sealed courtroom with no witnesses allowed. She took it.

Betty said before she left, "Judge, there is another thing I'd like to ask you. Courtrooms are public places. Usually divorces are public record. How come everything that has to do with Dan Broderick is secret and sealed?" He didn't answer.

Dan came in through the judge's entrance the day after Christmas, looking like he'd just stepped out of a magazine, a perfect red rose in his lapel. He was the past president of the bar, and Betty was the housewife in the jogging suit.

The judge said he wanted to review the entire case, the marriage, and all the assets in order to make his determination. "Do you remember this?" Betty would ask. "Do you remember that?"

"No," Dan would answer. All of a sudden he didn't remember anything. If Betty hadn't had his birth certificate, he wouldn't have remembered his name. She had to run home after court every day and collect the documents to verify the things he couldn't remember.

Luckily she had everything. Every receipt, every love letter, every picture of every event. That's just how she was. Betty showed it all to the judge. "Now do you remember?" she asked, challenging Dan each time. She was so furious and so tired from it all that she came down with fever, shakes, and laryngitis. "Can I have a day off?" Betty asked.

"No," the judge said. "We're almost finished."

They rushed her through her testimony. She ended up with the same sixteen thousand a month, but only until further order of the court. She still had no security. She got the stupid boat that was sinking. She had to pay someone to tow it away. She got Warner Springs, which wasn't paid for, and the piano, which wasn't paid for. She got half the value of the pension fund, but Dan said it was worth about a quarter of what it was really worth, and she couldn't touch that until she was sixty-five. Dan got to keep all the property and Dan was given custody of the kids. Betty got every other weekend and a month in the summer. "Shafted again," she said when it was over.

• 4 •

Betty Broderick on Dan's Legal Tactics

"Between 1983 and 1985 he maneuvered the money, the house, the car, and the checking accounts. The day he walked out, he just hit those dominoes, and I was out of business. Right down the line. And because I was laying low and trying to let him play out his crises, I was his perfect victim. I knew nothing about what he was doing with the money and the taxes and the debts. I knew nothing. He just set me up.

"He lowered our life-style. He didn't pay his income taxes. The day after he walks out, he writes checks for eight hundred thousand dollars to pay his back taxes, four hundred thousand dollars of that comes out of my community property. These are dangerous things for men to know because it was ingenious what he did.

"That day when he walked out, half of everything he had was mine. The day after he writes this check to the IRS, he pays off all these credit cards. He never settled the divorce for four years. He walked out in 1985. In 1986, '87, '88, and '89 I got no settlement. You know why? Every penny he's supporting the community with is coming out of my half. My half disappeared because he spent it. And I had no choice. Take, for instance, the ski condo. When he walked out, I owned half of the ski condo supposedly. Right? During these years that I have no settlement, he's making payments on that condo. He's able to use it anytime he wants. He's able to sell it because he has the paperwork and it's in his name. I am neither able to use it or sell it or get my money out of it. But he's making payments on this condo for all these years—out of my share. My entire 'community' disappeared.

"Every month that went by, he wrote checks for back debts from the

141

community property that wasn't split. The money he spent to pay off those debts, they're called Epstein credits. No one had ever heard of Epstein credits before. We lived on credit cards purposely for record keeping. I had a MasterCard, he had a Visa, and he had the gold American Express, which he did all the big traveling with. I also had every department-store credit card known to man. I lived on those. That's the way he liked the bookkeeping done. I never saw a dollar bill. Everything I did was plastic. That way he got to review every bill and everything I bought.

"Anyway, what he did unbeknownst to me, he started doing the minimum-credit-card-payment routine. By the time he walked out in 1985, we owed every card and every department store the maximum. He paid them after he walked out. Those debts come out of my half of the money.

"That son of a bitch was still paying Harvard Law School $89 a month in 1989, and he was still billing me for those monthly payments.

"In 1983 I was on top financially, socially, morally, and most importantly legally. He bought me a $2,500 overdraft protection on my checking account. The day he walked out, $2,500 was overdrawn on that account. He knew I had no checks to write. I couldn't write anything. He made sure there was no money there. Then he canceled my credit cards. He knew my name wasn't on a copper penny. I didn't even have a teacup with money in it at home.

"Then there were all the little tricks. The boat, for example, was a small ski boat. The whole time during the divorce he wouldn't let me use it. Anytime he wanted to use the boat, he could go use it. Anytime he wanted to sell the boat, he could go sell it. I could neither use it nor sell it. But I was fully supporting fifty percent of it. Dan didn't want to use it. He bought a great big new yacht. But he was going to keep it from me. He didn't want it, but he was going to be goddamned if I was going to get it. I would have liked the boat. The children and I used the boat. He didn't use it. He wanted a big yacht. It was so destructive to me and the children and to him and the property. It was just ridiculous.

142

"All those legal letters that he would write me were setting me up for the domino game. He would use precise legal language telling me that on this date this would happen, on that date that would happen. I didn't know any of these things could happen. I never heard of bifurcation. I never heard of a fucking Epstein credit. I never heard of one parent getting sole custody, no visitation, at a hearing where nobody was present. I never heard of such a thing.

"Dan tormented me legally. Imagine him wanting half of $89.

"I didn't know what could happen. He knew perfectly well. He had the whole thing right in his pocket. What had been my half in 1985 was spent by the time we got to 1989. I got literally nothing. I got $28,000 plus the piano that had debt on it. The boat that had debt on it and Warner Springs had debt on it. So if you add up those three debts, plus the $100,000 I spent on lawyers, I got minus $80,000 in this divorce. That was my half of millions.

"In the movie for television they didn't even mention that Dan and Linda were having an affair. How do you tell this story and leave that out? Please! And they advertised it as the truth, *The Betty Broderick Story*. They never even talked to me.

"It was Dan's version that he was married to this crazy wife who was doing these stupid things and bouncing off the walls. And of course he and Linda were just the innocent, nice people that were minding their own business. Huh! How come everything was sealed up? How come everything disappeared? How come there was no record of anything? Dan had real power. The legal system was his weapon, and I was the biggest case he was ever going to win.

"Yes, I called Linda Kolkena a cunt, big fucking deal. I was trying to fight back. I didn't even start doing that until years into this thing, as a self-defense mechanism when I was desperate. That's what Dan and Linda had against me. That I called Linda a cunt.

"Even now, even three years later when I'm here in prison, I'm still trying to intellectualize it. As soon as I start talking from my heart, I die. That's why you scared me when you said you wanted to talk about the kids. I can't talk about the kids very much because that's a whole other realm. As long as I stay angry about the money and the legal system, and about Linda being such a bitch, as long as I stay angry, I'm okay. But as soon as I talk about the real hurt of it, not the anger but the hurt, oh my God, it's nothing I can cover up.

• 5 •

Betty found a job teaching in a nursery school. It made her feel like she was functioning. She still loved kids. "I'm finally back on my feet," she told Brad.

One day someone kept calling the nursery school asking for her. As soon as she anwered the phone, the person hung up. After the fourth time Betty got a very weird feeling that something was up. She rushed home. Maria met her at the door. "Two ladies were in the house when I got here," Maria said in broken English. She described Linda and someone else whom Betty didn't recognize. "The pretty one with the long blond hair said she was a friend of yours. She had to pick up papers for you. She was in your room a long time looking in all in your closets and everything."

Betty walked upstairs. Linda had taken her diary and some legal papers. *She must have been calling to make sure I was at work,* Betty thought. She ran to the courthouse. It was locked, but she found the judge in his chambers. "Linda Kolkena has just broken into my house and taken my diary and legal papers," she said.

"Well, Mrs. Broderick," he announced. "You have the full power of the court to avail yourself of. You can get restraining orders against Linda."

Yeah, right, a lot of good that will do me, she thought. Suddenly Betty felt weary. "I won't be bothered," she said haughtily. "Please. Why would I be bothered? She can have the whole fucking room full of legal papers because nobody needs legal papers anyhow. Nothing I do ever stops them. I'm completely at their mercy."

Betty went straight from the courthouse over to Weisser's gun place next to the freeway. The man in the store showed Betty some guns. He had her try a few out to see which one she liked best.

Betty was in the stall at the very west end of the range. Next to her a man was having a lesson. "That lady's a hell of a shot," the man's teacher said. "Look at that. Her whole cluster was within the bull's-eye."

"You're doing very well," the man told her, walking over to Betty and striking up a conversation.

"I took lessons a zillion years ago in high school," she said, smiling. "I guess I still remember." The man introduced himself and told her he was a lawyer. "Oh," Betty said. "I'm married to a lawyer. I mean, I used to be."

"Who?" the man asked.

"Dan Broderick," Betty answered.

"I know Dan. Say hello for me." That was the extent of it.

Betty bought a .38 and three boxes of hollow-tipped bullets. *I can't defend myself in court and I can't defend myself at home, either, if I have nothing to defend myself with,* she thought. *The next time one of them assaults me or breaks into my house, I'm going to have something to defend myself with. I'm pretty goddamn sick of it. This divorce was supposed to be over, done, finished. Dan and Linda are getting married in April. What is wrong with these people? They've already arrested me. They've thrown me in jail and they've thrown me into a mental institution. Why won't they just leave me alone?*

• 6 •

First the gun was in the plastic case. It had a metal clip, and Betty hung it in the closet between the clothes. It was very important to Betty that there not be an accident. She instructed Danny, Rhett,

145

Kim, and Lee to stay away. "This is a real gun," she said. "Don't touch it, ever. Don't fool around with it. Under penalty of death, do not touch this gun."

When Betty left the room, Danny grabbed the gun and ran outside sobbing. He wanted to hide it from Betty so that she couldn't kill Dan. Betty panicked. She just went crazy. "My God, Danny," she yelled when she found him. "Don't you ever in your life touch that. I'm not kidding. Not only the gun. You're not allowed to touch the case."

After that Betty was always paranoid about where the gun was when the boys were in the house. She tried keeping it in the nightstand with the little drawer because that's where she thought people kept guns. She wasn't comfortable with it there. It was too easy to get to. Next Betty tried the top drawer of the built-in lingerie unit at the foot of her bed. She was still worried. Finally she decided to keep it in her pocket or in her purse.

Since Danny and Rhett were both fascinated with the gun, Betty figured that this was the one way to make sure that they wouldn't get their hands on it.

On Sunday when Dan came over to get the boys, Danny was so scared that he held on to her, kept hugging her, pressing his body against hers so that she couldn't reach into her pocket.

As the boys were getting into the car, Betty said to Dan, "Danny caused a lot of trouble over the weekend. Ask him to tell you about it."

"She bought a gun, Daddy," Danny said, crying. "I think she's gonna kill you and then kill herself. I tried to take it. I told my friend Matt about it. Now Mom's mad at me."

"Don't worry," Dan said. "Your mother's been making threats for years. She always says, 'I'll kill you' whenever she's mad at somebody. She won't do anything."

"You're wrong, Daddy," Danny insisted. "I know you're wrong."

146

Linda bumped into Steve Kelly in the mall. He looked as good as ever. The same old flame rose up between them. Nothing had really changed.

She followed Steve back to his place and made love all afternoon. Just like old times. It gave Steve a strange feeling to think that now Linda was betraying Dan Broderick with him.

"Betty's a loon," Linda said afterward when they were resting quietly. "She never stops."

"Linda," Steve said. "Ex-wives are like tattoos. They don't go away."

"If we make life hard enough for her, maybe she'll disappear." Linda said. Then her voice began to quiver. She seemed to be scared of Betty and to be egging her on at the same time. Sometimes it seemed like she was daring the devil. "We're a law office," Linda said. "It doesn't cost us anything to harass her."

"I still wish you'd leave him," Steve said softly.

"We're getting married in April," Linda whispered. "I'm sorry," she added when she looked into Steve's eyes.

"People are afraid to come to the wedding," Linda told her friend Eileen a few days later. They were on the way to Costa Mesa for a wedding-gown fitting. "They're afraid they'll be shot. We've been practicing hitting the dirt in case there's gunfire."

"Oh, come on," Eileen said, trying to lighten things up. "If a car backfires, I bet you guys will hit the dirt and ruin your clothes."

When they stopped for lunch at a small off-the-street café in La Jolla, Linda insisted on a dark corner table two jumps from the ladies' room. She said she was terrified to be in Betty's neighborhood. "If I see her coming," Linda added, "I'll dash into the bathroom and lock myself in while you run to the phone and call the police."

• 8 •

The day before the wedding Helen Picard got nervous. She called
Jeanne Milliken. Jeanne's husband was the judge marrying them.
"Betty called me at six A.M.," Helen said. "She was comparing her
own wedding with Dan and Linda's. She wants to buy an expensive
new watch for herself and have it engraved with Dan and Linda's
wedding date. We have to do something."

Jeanne tried to reach Dan and Linda, then she called Helen back.
"I couldn't get them," she said.

Helen took money out of the bank. She called Betty. "Let's go to
Palm Desert for the weekend so you won't have to think about the
wedding," she suggested.

"First off," Betty answered, "I don't care about the wedding, and
second off, tell me why, because I've never understood why anyone
would drive from La Jolla to Palm Desert. What could we do there?"

"Well," Helen said. "We could sit around the pool at the hotel."

"That's boring. I have a pool right here with an ocean view, my own
kitchen, my own champagne, my own bathroom, and my own down
comforter. What the hell would I drive to a fucking motel in Palm
Desert for? I've never been to Palm Desert because I don't want to go
there. Is it a thrill for you to sit around a motel pool? Are you out of
your mind? I'm going to drive two and a half hours to sit by that pool
when I can sit right here? No thanks. I don't want to go. I don't want
to go. I don't want to go. Besides, I want to be here in case my kids
call."

Helen kept hounding her.

"Look, Helen," Betty finally said. "There's no way I'm going. If you
want to take the weekend off, you can come stay with me. My home
is better than any hotel you can afford, honey. It's on the ocean and
it's got everything primo. It's better than the Ritz Carlton, my house."

"Okay," Helen said. "I'll come in the morning at seven o'clock and
spend the day with you."

As soon as she got off the phone, Helen drove over to Jeanne

148

Miliken's. "Here's a beeper," she said. "If Betty gets away from me, the beeper's going to go off. It's all I can do. Tell Dan and Linda it's my wedding present to them."

Helen packed her little bag and drove over to Betty's at six forty-five. Betty was awake and looking through her own wedding album. "Who's this? What's that?" Helen kept saying.

Betty thought Helen was acting very weird. She kept following her around the house. She even kept the bathroom door open when she went in to pee and kept talking to Betty the whole time, as if she were keeping an eye on her.

The weather was beautiful, perfect for a drive in Betty's little convertible. But Helen was afraid she'd take off and break for Dan's. "Let's take my car. I'm just in the mood to drive," Helen said.

"What the hell," Betty answered. She agreed to go and see Helen's kids at the YMCA baseball game.

She must have seen two hundred people there that she knew. It was like a big social thing with all the families she hadn't seen since she lost the kids.

On the way home Betty pointed to a pickup truck that had been parked across from her house. "We're being followed," she said.

"Don't be paranoid," Helen answered wishing Dan had told his security men to be more discreet.

When they got back, Gail Forbes came over. Her husband was not only Dan's law partner, they were best friends. Gail was a supermom to five kids, not flashy at all. She came from a very rich San Francisco family. She was as close a friend as Betty had. "It was no big deal," Gail said, playing the wedding down.

Brad showed up and wanted to go to dinner. "No," Betty said. "I'm still waiting for my kids to call."

Then Dan's sister rang the bell. "Everyone tells me you're crazy," she said. "I didn't believe it, so I decided to come over and see for myself." Betty filled her in. "Oh, I'm so sorry," Dan's sister kept saying. "He never could have gotten away with it if you were still on the East Coast."

"Don't feel bad," Betty told her. "Living back there, how could you know?"

Finally the kids called. "It was really honky," Kim whispered. "You should see all her low-class friends."

"It wasn't even a real wedding," Rhett said, taking the phone. "It was just a bunch of people standing around on Daddy's front lawn with his friend marrying him. Really, Mom, who ever heard of getting married by your own friend?"

• 9 •

Betty Broderick on Dan's Emotional Tactics

"He could have married any day of the year, but he married right on our twentieth anniversary. Dan did things like that to hurt me. Their honeymoon on the boat with sails is another example. He knew I wanted to go on that boat for four or five years. He could have gone anywhere in the world on his honeymoon, but he chose that boat with the sails thinking it was the one I wanted to go on. Turned out he picked the wrong boat. The boat I wanted to go on was the *Sea Cloud*. But all he knew it as was the boat with the sails. That's what I kept saying. Then they invented these new ones that he went on, the Windjammers with the computerized sails. So he tells the kids, the kids tell me, he's going on the boat with the sails, and I say, 'Oh, my God.'

"The Windjammers are big commercial boats. Expensive, don't get me wrong, but the *Sea Cloud* is the absolute luxury. It was the private yacht of Marjorie Merriweather and E. F. Hutton when they were married. It's real small, only fifty people can get on this boat. Dan and Linda went on one of these big things, but it had sails.

"I wanted a green ring for Christmas, but I didn't get it. I have never seen the ring he got Linda, but guess what, it was green. My favorite colors have always been blue and burgundy. Our entire house was blue and burgundy. When we were marrried, I wanted Dansk dishes. We couldn't afford them. And I didn't get them, but I always wanted Dansk. Guess what he put in his kitchen? The exact Dansk dishes that I wanted when we were married. He went back and got everything I ever wanted.

"I always wanted a grandfather clock. One of the first things he bought was a grandfather clock. These were things that we were going

151

to get as a couple when we moved to our bigger custom home, that we planned on for seventeen years.

"We got on a schedule and what happened was he went forward on the exact same schedule. I just got bumped off and replaced with someone that looked like me. It wasn't that he changed schedules and wanted a different life-style. He wanted the same life we always had. He just wanted a younger wife to put up with all his shit. A wife who would have five more babies. He had to have nine babies, just like his father."

• 10 •

Betty wanted the boys, and they wanted her. On Sundays Dan was supposed to pick them up at four or five. From ten o'clock on they were in a panic. "Oh, my God, he's coming, he's coming," they'd say each time a car went down the road. They'd be looking at the clock every hour.

On Father's Day Dan called Danny from his car phone to make sure he'd be waiting outside. The next thing Betty knew, Dan was there at the door. There was no Danny. Only a note. "I'm running away," it said. "I'll be okay. I'll call you at eight or ten to tell you I'm okay." At the end of the note it said, "Happy Father's Day."

Helen Picard marched in. "Don't worry, Dan," she said. "I'll find him for you." "Helen, I think you'd better leave," Betty whispered. "This has nothing to do with you." Helen ignored her. Dan called Danny. Helen called Danny. There was no answer.

Dan left, furious. Even Helen finally gave up. Betty sat on the stoop until dark. "Danny," she called, rustling the bushes as she walked. There were lots of bushes and trees. "Danny, I swear to God, he's gone, honey. Can you hear me? Please come out. Daddy's gone."

Finally Danny came out. "Let's go home," Betty said, hugging him.

Danny was so afraid that Dan would come back and find him in the house and have Betty arrested that he was shaking all over.

Finally Betty said, "Here's a deal for you. You sleep in Maria's room in the garage. You know, there's a nice little bed in there. It's a lovely room, and if Daddy or the police come to the door, I'll say, 'No, he's not in my house,' because you really won't be in my house."

Even so, neither one of them slept a wink all night. They expected the police any minute.

"Dan," Betty said, when Danny finally went home. "How many times and how many ways do these boys have to tell you they don't want to be there? They want to be with their mother."

Rhett had been telling Dan every day for years. Once, when Betty drove up to the soccer field, Dan had also just pulled up in his Jaguar. Rhett didn't want to go with Dan. He tried to run. Dan tackled him and threw him over his shoulder. Rhett began to shout, "Mom, Mom, help me, Mom. Please, help, help." He was kicking and yelling and crying. All the other parents were watching Dan. Dan had sole custody. Betty couldn't do a thing.

Whenever they were together for a night, the kids couldn't get enough of Betty. They would both climb into bed with her. She had to lie flat on her back because if she turned to one side or the other, the kid who got her back would get mad.

When they fell asleep, she'd sneak out of her own queen-size bed into one of their little beds just so she could get some sleep. In the morning when she woke up, both boys would be back in the twin bed with her and Betty would be holding on so she wouldn't fall off.

Once when Brad had been sleeping in Rhett's room, he heard the three of them laughing in Danny's bed. He came and jumped right on top of them, almost scared Betty to death. "This goddamn itty-bitty Ethan Allen bed is going to break into little splinters," she said. Then they laughed till their sides ached.

Dan never did that kind of thing. He was always too hung over in the morning.

• 11 •

Betty Broderick on Dan and the Kids

"He was being mean to the boys, but he wouldn't let me have them. He wouldn't let them come live with me. He threw both of the girls out of the house at eighteen with no education, no rent money, no cars. These kids did not belong in the street at eighteen, so I'm financing Lee and her boyfriend. I'm financing both of their cars. I'm financing Kim's education and Kim's clothing. I'm writing checks up the wazoo. You see, those two are over eighteen. He gave up custody at eighteen, because now I couldn't get child support. He knew I wasn't going to let them go out in the street and go hungry. He knew I was going to fully support them out of money that was not meant to support them. But if I got the boys, he would still have to give me child support, and he wouldn't do it.

"Again, in the kitchen that morning I'm thinking, you know, he's going to play this game with the boys until they're eighteen and then he's going to throw them out in the street. They're going to have dropped out of school and have all kinds of emotional problems and be on drugs like Lee. I'm going to get no college money for them either. That's what he did with the girls. I'm not making this up. I'm not delusional. He did it with the girls. And I could see him doing it with the boys too.

"The kids knew that I would do anything for them. I was a sucker, and sometimes they took real advantage of it, especially Kim. Kim really played me off right till the end there. She would call me all the time and say, 'Daddy and Linda this, and Daddy and Linda that,' and I would say, 'It's okay, Kim, it's okay. I'll take care of it. I'll write you the check.' And then I'd hang up the phone and say, 'That son of a bitch, treating my daughter like that.'

155

"You know that last phone call from her, three days before this happened, was that she had nothing to eat and nowhere to live and that her daddy wouldn't give her any money for college. I was so mad at him. How dare he treat our child like that.

"We had put her through all that private school so that she would have a fine college education. She was on the threshold of that, and he wouldn't pay for it. I was furius at him.

"All she had to say was, 'Daddy's being mean to me, Daddy won't buy me this, and Daddy won't buy me that, and Linda's such a bitch, and Linda this and Linda that,' and I'd say, 'Oh, honey, it's okay. Don't worry about it, I'll take care of it,' and then I'd write big checks and make her feel better because I felt so terrible. I was tired, just tired of everything. Tired of being without the kids, tired of the phone machine, tired of him manipulating the money, tired of being threatened with jail, of being threatened with this, being threatened with that. I was just tired."

• 12 •

In July they'd finally have a whole month together. Betty promised the boys they could take a trip. Then she ended up losing half of July preparing for a new custody fight with Walter Maund, her new lawyer. "It'll be worth it," she told the boys, " 'cause this time we'll win."

After they'd finished with two new psychiatrists, they drove up to Whistler Mountain in Canada. They fished and horseback rode. They drove past Vancouver, all the way up the coast and all the way back down. They skied on a glacier and did the dunes in Oregon. They stopped in San Francisco. It gave them a sense of freedom. Just like the good old days. It was perfect. No one knew that it was their good-bye trip.

From September to November it was straight downhill.

Both doctors recommended that Betty get the boys. They said she absolutely was not crazy. "Yes, she got mad," Gary De Voss said. "But who wouldn't."

The other psychiatrist concurred. Betty promised the boys they would be with her by September when school started.

Dan came back from a trip to Hawaii with Linda and put it off again. He said he personally needed to depose the doctors. It was the end of August. September came, school started. One more lawyer and one more humongous chunk of money wasted. One more promise made and broken. All for nothing.

The children had been counting on it. Betty had been counting on it. She had failed them again. Betty believed that this deadline, this school year, this effort was the last one. If Dan was still playing games now after the divorce, after the settlement, after the psychiatrists, after his marriage to Linda, then she would never win.

She was just wasting money on the big house with all the bedrooms and the swimming pool. It ate up her discretionary money and gave her no enjoyment. She was lonely in that house. All it did was remind her that she was alone in a neighborhood filled with families and kids. Every day that Betty lived there without those boys just heightened her sense of loss.

"Okay," she said. "I give up. I'll sell the house. I'll be a single person. I'll sell the Chevy Suburban. I'll buy a condo and a little two-seater Mercedes. The mortgage will be low. I'll have money to travel and dress."

She found a condo in La Jolla and bought it. Her mortgage would be less than half of what it was in the house. No outside maintenance, no grounds, no pool. On paper it made perfect sense. Inside she was crumbling.

Brad suggested Acapulco. It would take her mind off things. He made her promise that she would not back out, even if the kids showed up.

"No problem," she told him. "The weekends are all prearranged now."

In the past as soon as Dan heard she had plans, he would say, "Okay, you can go to Mom's that weekend." If she didn't have any plans and just sat home crying, Dan didn't let them come.

"I promise you, Brad," Betty said. "No more of that. There's a divorce now. There's a calendar of every other weekend. It's settled, it's over, I will not back out of the trip."

The next week, without telling her, Dan went to court and made a deal to change the weekend so that he could take the kids and Linda to the big Notre Dame game in South Bend. On alternate years the game was held in California. They had attended that, but this fall weekend at Notre Dame went all the way back to the core of Betty's dream. Dan had always promised that someday they'd have enough money to fly out there with all the kids and go to that game, but somehow they never did.

This was the first time the entire Broderick family was going to celebrate their heritage. The entire family, except for Betty. It was an event she had looked forward to since the day she was married.

Betty had a history with these people that went back to high school. And here's this brand-new stranger who looks like her with her husband and her kids.

She went to Warner Springs Ranch to get away from it. But she couldn't do it. There was no TV in the house, so she went to the restaurant and bar to watch the game.

A nice young woman with a stroller and a bunch of kids was waiting while her husband watched the Notre Dame game on the TV. It turned out he had also gone to Notre Dame.

"You remind me of me when my kids were small," Betty said. "They're at that game right now. I wonder how cold and how rainy it is. You know, anything can happen in South Bend in October. I wonder if I sent them in the right clothes."

Betty wanted her girls to look better than Linda because it was the first time their friends were meeting the kids. She bought Kim a six-hundred-dollar Ralph Lauren leather jacket, a navy-blue sweater, plaid pants, and new shoes. Betty was sure Kim looked a lot classier than Linda Kolkena would ever look.

All the kids had new outfits. They all looked great. But Betty wanted to be there herself to meet her old friends. To be the mother of the family that she had raised.

She had sixteen thousand dollars a month now, but what good was it if she couldn't get on a plane and join them? She could buy all the plane tickets and football tickets and clothes she wanted, but she couldn't join them. She was out of the family that she spent her whole life building. She couldn't just fly there and go as herself and say, "Hi, everybody, I'm here."

So she sat at the bar and told these strangers how old her kids were and what each of them was like. "Why aren't you there with them?" the girl asked.

"Well, my husband married his secretary," Betty answered, "and she's there with my kids."

"Oh, that's very sad," the girl said. She didn't ask too many questions because she was buried in her own little kids; the baby in the stroller was still in diapers. A mother with litle children is a very busy person. Betty could see that she was very loving and supportive of her husband. She was devoting her life to that husband and those children and she was very happy doing it.

Betty smiled at the girl. *When those kids grow up and that husband has enough money to go to Notre Dame games, I want her to go with them, Betty thought, because she earned it and she belongs there.*

• 13 •

They went to Acapulco with a group. Brad sailed all day and talked about boats. He needed a companion for dinner, and Betty was good for that. During the day she'd shop or sit by the pool because she didn't sail.

She got to meet lots of people, and soon they all knew that she and Brad were really good friends. They went everywhere together.

Actually he was free to meet other people and Betty was free to meet other people on all these trips, totally free to meet other new people if that so happened.

She trusted Brad enough to know that he was a lovely person and wouldn't do anything blatantly rude. If he met a really nice girl, he'd exchange phone numbers or addresses or something. He'd get together with that girl the next day or the next time. But he wouldn't leave Betty stranded. He would not ignore her the whole night. He did it the way civilized people did these things. She could count on him for that. It was okay with Betty. He was too young. They were never going to end up together. He was a good, fun person to spend time with, but he didn't want to marry her.

Before she'd bought the condo, Betty had swallowed her pride. She'd asked him about getting married or possibly just moving in together, maybe buying a place on Point Loma together, on the water, where he could keep his boat.

If they got married, she'd lose her entire settlement. That's how Dan had set it up. No more money if she remarried. Not a dime. Then if that new guy left her, that would be it. Still she asked Brad if he'd like to. He just smiled and said nothing. Betty wasn't surprised. That was always how Brad said no.

Actually Betty couldn't figure out why he kept wanting to go on all these stupid trips with her. "Why don't you invite someone you can have a future with? Why don't you find a young girl and get married and have babies and be a real person, be a normal person?"

Betty knew Brad couldn't provide her with what she needed. At the same time Betty was now free to form a new relationship. As free as she was ever going to be. But she couldn't get what she longed for anywhere except from her kids and from Dan. No, thank you. No men, no sex, no love, no furs, no condos, no cars, no nothing could do that for her.

If a man could have done that for her, she would have married some rich guy right back in the beginning and moved somewhere else and gone about her business.

She didn't fit in with the wives on this trip, and she didn't fit in with the girls on dates who were walking around with their boobs hanging

160

out and acting like dates do. She wasn't comfortable in a public hotel in the same room as Brad. She didn't need to shop and she was bored on the beach. "I'm a misfit, Brad," she said. "I'm very depressed."

As soon as she got home, Betty tried to reach her children. It was clearer to her than ever that the relationship with Brad wasn't going anywhere. Her kids were all she had, all she lived for. They had been calling. She saw their messages. She called them. "This is the Broderick residence. We can't talk to you now," Linda chirped.

"I don't believe this," Betty said. "The judge told them no more girlfriend on the machine, but now that she's his wife, she's back on the line again. She does this just to torment me. What other reason would she have to be interfering with what little contact I have left with my children?" Betty slammed down the phone. *I'll probably get in trouble for this,* she thought as she picked it up and dialed again.

"Rhetty Pooh . . . Hey, Rhett," she said. "Why can't you hear this? Has the cunt been playing with the phone again?" The tears felt hot on her cheeks. "This really amuses me, that she has nothing else to do after all this time but play with the stupid phone. Marriage must be great. Ha."

Betty looked at her watch. "Well, let me see here. It's seven o'clock. You called last night. You need to know something. If you get this message, call me at the house and I'll tell you whatever it is you need to now. Okay, poops? 'Bye."

Betty poured herself a cup of coffee and looked at the clock. *That bitch really knows how to get to me,* she thought. It was still too early for the boys to have left for school. Betty missed those boys. She missed her babies. She picked up the phone and dialed again.

"Danny, it's Mom. I know you guys are down there, unless the cunt turned the ringer off again. Danny, what did you want last night, honey? Next time you guys want something, just tell my machine and then whenever I get home, I'll tell your machine the answer, okay? Anyway I'm at the house if you get this message. 'Bye."

• 14 •

Betty Broderick on Dan and Linda's Emotional Tactics

"No one ever called Linda or Dan at that number. They had office phones, car phones, cellular phones, and the other phone number at the house. That was the kids' phone. Dan had court orders to keep her off the phone. There was not a single phone incident in all of '88 or '89 until she got back on the phone. Why was she playing games with my life and my children? So many times I said, 'Please, do not torment me and drive me crazy and threaten me with things.' In 1989 I'd had it.

"What did they finally hope to achieve? To have me kill myself or drive myself crazy? They humiliated me daily. They just chipped away at every aspect of my life. They were relentless, both of them. Dan was relentless legally, and she was relentless emotionally. Linda put her voice on my kids' answering machine. Linda broke in and stole my diary and legal papers. Linda sent me the note that said, 'Eat your heart out bitch,' along with the pictures of them at the Blackstone Ball. They were not going to stop until I was dead. Until Dan didn't have to give me a cent of anything and till I couldn't call my kids. I felt like they wanted to see me eradicated from the face of the earth, to want no money, no support, to not want any contact, even telephone calls to my children. I said it in court. I said, 'I stood in my kitchen the morning that it happened and said, "God, take me away from this. I can't stand it another minute." ' But God didn't take me. As long as I was here, I had certain needs, wants, rights, and desires. To the kids primarily. Did Linda think she was honestly going to keep me from talking to my kids in 1989? My visitation was now only every other short weekend, and she was going to play her games and she was going to expect me not to talk to them. Wrong. Very wrong. She had no right to fuss about the phone ringing.

"I just got more and more depressed. I was supposed to get on with my life, but without my children I had no life.

"I just wanted to die. I just wanted it to go away, the pain of this struggle."

• 15 •

Betty hadn't seen the kids for three weeks. When she finally saw them, it was going to be for such a short time that all she could do was cry. The kids were going to be worried starting at ten o'clock on Sunday morning that Dan was going to come.

Danny wanted to go to Tijuana, but she'd have to call Dan and ask if she could keep them later than five. Depending on what Dan's mood was, he could say yes or no and control their whole day. That was the way it always was.

She was in the process of moving to the condo, and the depression was building. It was deepening and deepening and deepening until Betty was at the absolutely blackest lowest point of despair she thought she could be and still be alive.

She couldn't stop crying. She saw no end in sight and nowhere to go for relief or help. Blackness everywhere, the lights had gone out. She looked at the beautiful house with the beautiful view and she didn't see it anymore.

She cried watching Rhett at the soccer field because he didn't know how to play the game and because he had lost so much.

New legal papers had just arrived from Dan. They were at home on the counter. She was afraid to read them. She knew Dan was never going to give her custody.

Saturday night Brad came over. Betty was so upset and depressed that she couldn't remember what she did from hour to hour.

She went to bed at five-thirty or six because she couldn't move, just lay on top of her bed with her clothes on. She wasn't really planning to sleep. Brad stayed up with the boys. When she awakened at dawn, she didn't realize Brad was still there. She didn't care really. He was going sailing on Sunday, they were going to Tijuana if Dan would let them. Betty still had not read those legal papers, but she knew they weren't good news. She had never yet gotten legal papers from Dan that said, "Congratulations, you've won." She figured it was more of the same.

Betty glanced at the Holy Card on her refrigerator. "God will not give you more than you can handle," it said. She picked up the letter and began to read. It was addressed to her new lawyer. Betty's eyes darted across the page, scanning it: "Enclosed please find a verbatim transcript of just a few of this week's obscene messages left on my client's answering machine."

"As you know," the letter continued, "respondent was ordered to pay $26,000 in penalties and was sentenced to 28 days in jail for various contempt violations in the past. I firmly believe another jail sentence will be imposed." Betty turned white and began to shake. Her eyes raced to the end of the letter. It said, "I find respondent's actions completely inconsistent with the contentions of her psycho-therapists that her emotional disturbance and mental disease are improving. The contrary appears to be the case."

Betty sat frozen, as if she had just been wiped out on the spot. Slowly she picked up a pen and began to write: "I can't take this anymore. (1) Linda Kolkena, the cunt, interfering with what little contact I have left with my children. She's been doing it for years. We're litigating it continuously. (2) Constant threats of court, jail, contempt, fines, etc. Which is very scary to me and no matter what the evidence I always lose. (3) Them constantly insinuating I'm crazy."

She put down the pen. *I'll kill myself,* she thought very calmly. *It's the only way out. I'll go down to the beach and kill myself. Oh, God, no,* she cried. Danny and Rhett will be so badly hurt, so lost if I do that. Suddenly she couldn't breathe.

She ran outside and jumped into the car. *I'll go to the beach and get some air,* she thought, her head throbbing. *No, no, I'll go to Dan's. I'll*

165

*try to talk to Dan one last time. I'll ask him for the boys. If he won't agree,
I'll kill myself at his house, not down at the beach, and not in my house. I'll
splash my brains all over his fucking house so he can't say, "See, I told you
she was crazy. I had nothing to do with it."*

*I'll take the gun to make him listen to me. If he says "I'm going to call
the police," I'll say, "Oh, no, you're not. This time you're going to hear me
out."*

There were a lot of thoughts churning around inside Betty's head.
It felt as if the whole world was rolling around in there. A lot of
anguish and darkness. She kept thinking about the legal papers,
about being fined again and going to jail again.

Betty had Kim's keys with her. She tried the front door. The keys
didn't work. She walked around to the back and opened the door. She
climbed the stairs with the gun in her hand. After that Betty couldn't
remember much. It was like a slide show with some of the slides
missing.

• 16 •

Helen Picard couldn't stop screaming. "Why are you blaming
Betty?" she kept saying to Walter Maund. "She's in Tijuana with
Danny."

"No," he told her. "She doesn't have the boys. They're at Gail
Forbes's house.

"Well," Helen said, "I'll go look for her and clear this mess up."

"The police want you to stay right there in the office," Maund said.
"Don't go anywhere. They're putting a police car at your house in
case she goes there. They're afraid she might try to take everyone out,
first kill the boys, then kill herself."

An employee in Helen's office called some of her friends to come
over and sit with her because she was hysterical. Six hours later they

were still there. Helen kept thinking about the morning before. She had stopped by to see the boys. Betty was in the middle of moving her stuff to the condo. She was in a hurry. She had to get the boys haircuts and go to a game. She invited Helen to join them and go to Tijuana the next day.

The letter from Dan's lawyer was on the counter. She asked Helen to read it. Neither of them picked it up. "You've never understood how bad it is," Betty said. She was so agitated about that letter that she burned the bagel she was toasting for Helen.

Another unusual thing happened. As Helen was leaving, Betty stopped and put her hand on Helen's shoulder. There was a sad look in her eyes. "Do you think Linda's pregnant?" she asked.

"How should I know," Helen answered, shrugging. "Anyhow, who cares?"

• 17 •

The cathedral was packed, over one thousand people had poured into Saint Joseph's to stare at the twin caskets covered with red roses for Dan and white roses for Linda. More flowers in the shape of a shamrock surrounded them.

Danny was looking straight ahead. Rhett was crying. Helen Picard walked over to Danny and bent down. She hugged him. "We both tried," she said. "We did our best."

"What we are here for is to console one another," Father Joe Carroll told the group. "And yet this is a celebration because we believe Dan and Linda have gone on to a better life." After that people took turns speaking. There was crying and there was laughing. Linda's sister said, "Linda was born on a summer day, and from that moment on it was as if we got an extra dose of sunshine." One of Linda's friends rambled on about chocolate-chip cookies.

"Our only hope is to come to grips with the loss to each one of us and to put aside the horror," Dan's friend Judge Enright said. "We do not and cannot understand the loss. We accept the will of God, but we grieve. Oh, how we grieve. May they rest in peace."

After the caskets were carried out, after the Irish flag and the Dutch flag flew, after the bagpipes played, after the friends and family and spectators had all left, Kim and Lee and Danny and Rhett walked out of the church. Kim sat down on the steps and sobbed. Lee put her arms around her. Danny held Rhett's hand. They were all alone.

PART VI

• • •

The Trials

"I thought life was a progression of steps. I took all the right steps. I learned all the good old rules. I thought that if you worked hard and told the truth and did the right things, everything worked out right. . . . Well, it didn't."

—*Betty Broderick phone call, September 1992*

• 1 •

It was a double metal bunk about the size of a parking space. There was a little wall in front of the toilet so that male guards couldn't watch. The skinny slant window was blackened so she couldn't see out.

In all of Section A of Las Calinas Prison the only world outside that Betty could see was a small patch of sky from inside the inner courtyard. Even that had chicken wire on top.

Twenty-four hours a day she could hear the screams of people withdrawing from drugs, mentally ill people, and violent cases. She was handcuffed, shackled, and chained before being led to the showers.

Betty was still shackled and lying on a cot with no pillow when her cellmate came in. Karen Wilkening, the notorious Rolodex Madam had been a fugitive in the Philippines for nearly two years before she was deported. When the plane landed in L.A., the cops were waiting. They arrested her, put her in waist chains and handcuffs, and locked her in a police car.

"You're facing up to twenty years in prison for pimping and parole violations," one of them said. She didn't answer.

"Hey, Karen, don't you recognize me?" he asked a few minutes later. "Me and my friend met you at one of them bachelor parties." She turned around this time. She did remember. She had provided dancers for a party for some vice cops and met two men there—this was the cop who had called to make the arrangements. It was his friend's name that police found in her Rolodex.

Now as he led her into the cell, Karen looked at Betty's tearstained face. "Hello," she said, reaching out her hand and smiling.

"Thank you," Betty answered, taking in Karen's kind expression. "I'll never forget your smile."

171

• 2 •

Mark Wolf did a little digging. He found out that Betty had a house that would probably sell for over a million dollars. She signed everything over to him. First he sold her house, then he took Dan's pension fund. When he told Betty that he had hired a publicist and a dresser to dress him for TV appearances, she began to worry.

A few weeks later Jack Earley showed up at Las Calinas. Betty figured he was shopping. "Hire me and I'll move the trial out of San Diego," he said. "I'll convince the jury that it was self-defense, a case of emotional abuse. I'll set you free."

"Wolf's got every dime," Betty told him.

"Don't worry about that," Earley said. "I'll collect the money from him. It will cost two hundred fifty thousand dollars to start."

Wolf turned it over to Earley. But he told Betty she already owed him almost two hundred thousand dollars. He was holding all the money. What could she do?

"Betty doesn't believe there is anyone in San Diego who would be able to take on the bench and the bar," Wolf explained to the press. "I can understand her feelings. Dan took her to the cleaners, and most of all, the legal system helped him to do that. . . . There is very little difference in this case from a battered-wife case. The only difference is that the two-by-four Dan Broderick used was the legal system."

Wolf was right. Dan had such a powerful legal reputation that people fought to get him. He had nearly two hundred cases pending when he died. He was the Killer Attorney. No one wanted to see him coming into the room from the other side.

Even now potential witnesses from San Diego were afraid to testify against him because it might affect their future. At least Jack Earley didn't have the San Diego pressures. He was based in Newport Beach, down the coast from Los Angeles. When he told her he specialized in homicide cases and had represented almost two dozen homicide clients as a public defender, she was hopeful.

172

On the prosecution side was Kerry Wells, a bright, tough, articulate graduate of Whittier College School of Law. Kerry Wells was chief of the Domestic Violence Unit, and this was the ultimate domestic violence.

It had been ten years since she had finished law school, but this was her first murder trial. The legal world had always been part of her life. She grew up with a dad who she thought was the greatest lawyer since Clarence Darrow, her absolute hero. She was the only girl in a family of three sons and glad about it. Kerry Wells liked competing in the male world. She was a jock in college and for a while she was considering a career in sports medicine.

During her senior year in college Kerry's best friend was murdered. She and her brand-new husband were both wiped out by someone who was never caught.

At the time that happened, Kerry was twenty-one years old and had never suffered a moment of tragedy. It had been a very blessed life. Suddenly everything else seemed trivial. She lost interest in doing anything at all.

Almost simultaneously Kerry met the man she ended up marrying. She needed someone then. She hung around Tucson, Arizona, an extra year doing nothing, floundering around, thinking about her murdered friend. It was not until her boyfriend finished law school and was being sworn in that she said to herself, "I know what I want to do. I want to be a prosecutor."

From that minute on she knew it was the right choice. She loved it. From day one of law school she waited for the time when she could prosecute her first big case, avenge her first murder.

After two years in the city attorney's office prosecuting misdemeanors and eight more years in the D.A.'s office working with victims of domestic violence, it was finally happening.

Kerry always knew she could kick butt with the boys. Her dad was real competitive. He always said, "Go get 'em, Kerry, you can do it." That's where her intensity and her passionate commitment to winning came from.

It wasn't until she went into Dan and Linda's house the day after the murder that her ambition, her energy, and her own bitter loss all

173

came together. Mostly it was the little things that got to her. The dirty dishes still unwashed in the kitchen sink, Linda's curlers and makeup, her toothbrush and her jewelry. Just like Kerry's friend, this had been a living, breathing woman, cut off in the bloom of her life.

The family wanted Linda's wedding dress to bury her in. Kerry had to search the closet before she found it sealed away in a box. Then she walked down the hall to the children's room to collect and pack the boys' clothing and toys. Kerry herself had two young sons.

Her own dad, her treasure, her main support, had recently died. Now he wasn't there to say, "Get 'em, Kerry." Just like Danny and Rhett, she had lost her dad. She missed him in the good times and the bad. She missed him now.

Kerry Wells had a mission. Her target was Betty Broderick.

• 3 •

Jack Earley was having trouble. Ten days before the pretrial hearing he filed a motion saying he wanted the entire San Diego D.A.'s office removed from the case. Earley also wanted to stop any local judge from hearing the case. He said none of them would be impartial. The trouble was no one was listening. Both motions were rejected, and Thomas Whelan was named to preside over the San Diego trial.

Like Kerry Wells it was Whelan's first time in a new role. He, too, had been a prosecutor. In more than twenty years he had lost only one case. People said he was a fair man and a righteous one. Seeing crimes avenged was his thing. Whelan claimed that his greatest weakness was that he was too sympathetic, a sucker for a sad story. But his strength, his secret of success, boiled down to a simple formula. On the surface he appeared calm, unruffled, like a duck, but beneath that surface he was always thinking and reacting.

With his thick gray hair swept back in a pompadour that crowned his square jaw and rugged face, Judge Whelan sat back in his big leather chair. He half closed his eyes and rocked occasionally. He listened impassively to nearly three weeks of jury selection.

When jury selection was over, 150 people had responded to more than 100 questions ranging from adultery to motherhood and murder. Two thirds of the jurors were eliminated right away. Six men, six women, and three alternates were finally chosen. The youngest was a nineteen-year-old girl who worked part-time in a tanning salon. There were three men in their sixties, two civilians who worked for the navy, and a county pollution inspector. There was also a teacher, a former preschool aide, a transit worker, a flight attendant, an executive, a Pacific Bell employee, a building contractor, and an industrial project manager.

• 4 •

More than a hundred people who couldn't get seats milled around in the long, dark hallway sipping coffee and eating snacks from the vending machines. They chatted and laughed as they watched Betty's trial on a TV monitor set up by a local station.

Jack Earley and Kerry Wells had both spent nearly a year preparing. They had gathered testimony, hired private investigators, interviewed potential witnesses, and practiced strategies for discrediting each other.

"This case," Kerry Wells said in her opening statement, "is about hate, revenge, and murder. It is about a woman who had so many things going for her that she could have done so much with—like a million-dollar home in La Jolla, like a sixteen-thousand-dollar-a-month income, like intelligence and education and friends, and four beautiful children, but none of it was enough because she was so consumed with hate."

It was a good opening. It got even better when Kerry described Betty entering the house to shoot Dan and Linda. Her voice rose, then fell and broke with emotion. She, too, was avenging a broken commandment. The jury felt her power.

Jack Earley also had a plan. He had worked on his opening statement. He hadn't memorized it as Wells had, but he'd thought about it. He'd even come up with a device that he thought would impress the jury. He stood up and walked toward a large white board mounted on an easel that had photographs of the Broderick family attached with Velcro. He ripped the photos off one by one to dramatize Betty's losses.

When only two were left, one of a gorgeous, thin, smiling Betty Broderick still with long blond hair taken in 1975 and the other a black-and-white photo of a fat, middle-aged woman taken in the late 1980s, Earley paused. He raised his arm and pointed to the second picture. This is what was left, he shouted at the jurors. "I think you'll see that it was someone who had no self-esteem. It was someone who had no way of dealing with problems, and I think you'll see that she was acting on emotions that were thrust on her."

Betty sobbed as Earley recounted her life with Dan. The birth of their children, their financial struggles, Linda's arrival, and Dan's tactics. "He started telling Elizabeth Broderick that she was crazy. She needed to be counseled," Earley said, "and that what she was seeing and what she was feeling wasn't really happening."

Earley also spoke about Dan's psychological campaign, his financial deceptions and legal strong-arming. As his last point he told the jury that Dan and Linda were awake when Betty shot them. "Someone yelled, 'Call the police,' and caused Betty to panic," he said. It was an important point, because it argued against premeditated, first-degree murder.

"Betty had not come over there to execute two people asleep in their beds," Earley told the jury as he wrapped up his opening statement. "She had merely come to talk to him, to try one more time before killing herself."

Kerry Wells started the people's case with practical details. After showing the jury the crime-scene photos, she brought the medical examiner in. "Linda died instantly, and Dan lived longer," she told the jury. Next a police firearms expert gave his opinion about the grievous nature of the hollow-point bullets that Betty fired. He also talked about the pattern of the shots. Now that she had their attention, Wells was ready to shock the jury. She played the obscene phone messages and took a break so that they could sink in, then Wells called Kim to the stand. Betty's own child, who was angry enough to speak against her, was one of Well's strong cards. Kim recalled talking to her mother on the morning of the shootings.

"I hung up the phone and called my dad's house, but there was no answer, and then I called the hospital. I called my friend. I called the police. I said, 'Has anyone been shot in Hillcrest on Cypress?' They said, 'Why do you ask? Who is this?' I said, 'It's Kim Broderick. Are they okay?' They said, 'We don't know what you're talking about. Where did you get this information?' I said, 'My mom told me.'"

It wasn't easy for Betty to listen to Kim up there. It brought back a lot of unhappy memories. Betty still didn't know why Kim had invited Linda to her high school graduation. Dan and Linda weren't married at the time. She was just his girlfriend. She didn't have any place there.

Had Kim forgotten that just three days before this happened, Dan told her that four hundred dollars a month was too much for an apartment and that she should find a roommate or get a cheaper place, even though he was making millions?

Had she forgotten how Dan had neglected the boys? That they were going to school with their shoes falling apart? Rhett's foot was touching the ground through the holes in his shoes. It was so bad, his teacher thought it was a safety hazard. He might fall down the stairs. Couldn't Kim understand that she didn't want them to be cold on rainy days? She didn't want her little sons to be the only kids in the whole class who were inappropriately dressed. They were young children. They needed someone there in the morning to ask if their teeth were brushed, if their hair was combed, if their homework was done.

Instead she'd go over there against court orders and find the maids in bed or sitting around drinking beer and watching TV. Then she'd get fined or arrested for trying to take care of her own children.

Had Kim forgotten the time the boys were left at the house alone and Danny had gone out on his bike and gotten hit by a car? Betty realized Kim wasn't a mother. She was just a kid herself. She didn't want her children to have to choose between their mother and their father. They were still married, they were still one family. Betty had never wanted to give Dan custody, but she wanted Kim to understand that she had dropped the kids off at their own house with their own rooms and their own father because the other house had rats in it.

She knew Kim loved her father. Christ, she loved him too. But he insulted both girls by telling them constantly that they didn't look good enough because they weren't blond and weren't thin enough. Those girls were practically anorexic trying to please him, when all the time it was the fault of his genes.

Betty's thoughts were interrupted by Kerry Wells marching in front of her with that straight-up-and-down man's walk, those eyes like nails.

"What else did she say about why she had done it?" Kerry asked.

"She didn't say why," Kim answered, sniffling as she spoke. "She just said, 'You know why,' and 'I need your support,' and 'He was making me miserable,' and 'I just couldn't stand to see how he was treating you,' and 'I couldn't go on living like this,' and then she was talking about the apartment in Arizona . . . that he wasn't giving me money. I was suffering at school . . . she couldn't bear to see the way he was treating me when he was going on vacations and I had no money to live."

This was not what Kerry Wells wanted the jury to hear. She paced for a minute, then changed the direction of her questioning.

"Did your mother ever express any remorse for killing your father?" she asked.

"No," Kim said, wiping her eyes.

"Did she ever say that she was sorry about what had happened?"

"No," Kim repeated.

"Did she ever say that it was an accident, that she didn't mean to do it?"

"No."

Kerry Wells glanced over at Betty, then back at the jurors. She

178

raised her eyebrows and adjusted her large horn-rimmed glasses. She pursed her lips.

"Can you tell us what names she would call Dan and Linda?"

" 'Fuckhead' and 'the Cunt,' " Kim answered.

"That was something she used often?" Kerry asked, glancing toward the jury again, to gauge their reaction.

"Yes," Kim answered.

And so it went with Kim on the stand for nearly five hours over two days, torn between tears and anger, alternately loving and condemning her mother.

• 5 •

Betty Broderick on the Children

"I don't know about Kim, what Kim's doing. When I talk to Kim or she writes me letters, it's as if nothing happened. I don't know how to gauge Kim. I just don't. All through jail and everything I have the letters from Kim. She thinks that there is absolutely nothing wrong between us. She takes the stand for Kerry Wells against me. She goes on television and says bad things. Then she gets on the airplane right after the *Oprah Winfrey* show and writes me a three-page letter from the plane saying she loves me and she's sorry she didn't have a chance to say more good things about me.

"The last years with Kim were the difficult teenage years. When she did things I didn't approve of, I let her know. We fought about them. Unfortunately that's what she seems to remember. I just don't know what to do with Kim.

"Lee I talk to every day. We are very close. Lee is fine. Lee is cool. She's extremely popular and pretty and very sensitive. She's very faithful to her boyfriends and she's a great kid. She has a very, very, very low self-esteem because Dan Broderick put her down for loving me. The day she left was the day he threw me in jail. She picked up and packed. She couldn't fight him. She felt so bad about what he did. She left trembling.

"Men do not focus on a marriage and family like women do. Mothers are the nurturers who hold the family together. The men concentrate on the money, life insurance, house payments, their jobs. That is their life. So when Dan Broderick took my children from me, it was like me taking his license to practice from him . . . worse, it's like me taking his legal cases and not knowing what to do with them and absolutely making a mess about the things he cared about so much. Rhett I talk to as much as I'm legally able. Danny—I don't have a very good picture of where he is because he went from the Brodericks' to Helen Picard's house, and I don't want to call there. But he wanted to be in La Jolla with his friends, and I respect his need.

"Rhett is with one of my brothers. He's happy. He doesn't have to listen to people tearing his mother apart. I talk to him once a week for fifteen minutes. The law didn't say fifteen minutes. It's the jail doing that. I'm allowed one phone call a week of a reasonable length. He's wonderful. But I haven't even spoken to this kid for a few hours yet since 1989. He's telling me stuff now for the first time that he's been trying to tell me since 1987, 1988.

"When you are talking about a mother and her children, there is something primal, there is some basic connection of blood and heart-beat. If my kids are hurt and in the emergency room, I would really rather it be me.

"I have no expectations anymore of how anything is going to be. I used to have a lot of expectations. I thought that if you did this, that happened next.

"I did everything the way the ideal mother and housewife and wife does it. I took it all to heart and I did it. I met the teachers. I knew the children's friends and their friends' mothers. I knew where they were. I had the parties. I did it all.

"That's why they were healthy and happy and honor students. They had wonderful self-esteem. They knew that I thought they were the center of the universe. They had self-esteem because their mommy loved them. After Dan took them, they were not the center of his universe at all. He was the center of his own universe.

"When people ask me today how my kids are, I say, 'You know what, it's over. It never would have been over before Dan Broderick decided that it was never going to be over. It didn't turn out well, but it's over.'

"All I had to look forward to in life, because it was the focus of my life, were my children. My children in school and my children's grad-uating and my children going to college and my children getting married and my grandchildren, because that was my life. Dan Broderick was going to make it difficult or impossible for me to experience my children's lives.

182

"Rhett was only four years old when this started. I have pictures. He still has the pot belly under his little polo shirt. He's at the merry-go-round at Balboa Park. And he looks so cute. This was just a little kid in saddle shoes, knee-high pants, and a little shirt.

"I told the court I cried at the soccer field the day before this happened. Rhett was running around on the soccer field not knowing what he was doing because he had missed three years of soccer that the other boys hadn't missed. I cried because of what this poor child had missed. He's been deprived of things that he should have had. Danny missed out too. I remember Danny got invited to go to Disneyland. I said, 'Danny, why didn't you go?' He said, 'Because, Mom, it's my day to see you. If I miss it, then I'll never see you.'

"I could never give up on my children and just go marry another man and forget my family happened. Nothing else was important to me. If I moved somewhere and had fancy clothes and a big social life and money and stuff, it had no meaning to me."

• 6 •

"She was real close to money," Helen Picard said. "It was the main goal in her life. She worshiped it."

Kerry Wells nodded approvingly. That was exactly what she wanted the jury to hear. Jack Earley just shook his head. Even after searching her own soul and trying to understand the truth at its core, Earley thought, she still didn't get it.

"Betty called me from prison and talked about them like they were still alive," Helen added. " 'She is destroying my life,' Betty said. 'She is destroying my family. She is destroying my children.' "

"What did you say in response to that?" Kerry asked.

"I said, 'So you destroyed her,' and she said, 'Yes.' "

After that Helen told the jury, she stopped taking calls from Betty. They were too painful.

For Kerry Wells it was another wonderful day. She'd done nothing but gain. Lee's testimony was brief. Kerry wasn't going to risk asking too much because she knew it could backfire. Lee looked at her mother. Her eyes clouded over. Betty smiled and nodded slightly.

Kerry stuck to the morning of the shooting. "Mom said she felt empty and dead inside and that she was so miserable she couldn't go on another day. She said that she had gotten a paper that said dad was going to put her in jail again. She asked me to go to her house and check on my brothers and make sure that they were okay."

This expression of interest in the children wasn't helpful. So Wells excused Lee.

Brad was next. Betty smiled again, and tears came to her eyes. Betty had never felt closer to him. Brad had stood by her through this ordeal. She would be grateful forever. As a gesture of thanks, she had signed over the condo to Brad, fully furnished.

It was just what Brad needed, a ready-made home. No commitments. He didn't have to do a thing except pick up his dirty underwear.

Brad smiled back at Betty. The tears in her eyes brought him back to the time when his mother was dying of cancer, after the radiation and chemotherapy had failed. Betty went to her side, to her deathbed, and sat with her. Betty held her hand, took care of her, and protected her.

Brad felt very connected to Betty after that, closer than he had ever felt to any woman except his mother. But sometimes he still couldn't reach her.

"Very frequently," Brad told the jury, "she would hide her feelings, you know, from her children and myself. . . . She would just sort of hibernate from everyone. If she couldn't be in good spirits, why, she just generally didn't like to have other people around."

Kerry glanced down at some notes. Then she went back to her goal of trying to establish premeditation for a first-degree conviction. "Have you heard her threaten to kill Dan and Linda in front of her children?" Kerry asked.

"Yes, I have," Brad admitted, "but she didn't repeat this on a daily basis. I heard it once in a while, not on numerous occasions."

184

"Were you aware of her keeping the gun in her pocket when Dan Broderick would come over to pick up the boys?"

"Yes, she did tell me that she did that a couple of times."

"You did think the extent of her anger was out of line, excessive, didn't you?" Kerry asked, pressing her advantage.

"Not necessarily, considering the circumstances," Brad answered.

"You talked to your mother about that," Kerry continued. "Your mother discussed with you that something needed to be done about her anger, the extent of her anger."

"Yeah, we talked about the circumstances," Brad said.

"So even your mother who was dying of cancer knew the whole story about the defendant's divorce, how angry she was to the point she talked about doing something about her anger."

"Yes," Brad acknowledged. "We talked about it."

Kerry's last witness was Ruth Roth, the psychologist who tried to mediate the custody dispute.

"I asked her to tell me how he had gotten custody of the children," Roth told the jury, looking down and reading from her notes. "She said that she was living in a house with no support and no money. There were rats in the house, so she took the children and their stuff to his house.

" 'He has everything now and the cunt,' she told me.

"When I asked her about her goals for custody, she said, 'I'm not going to be the single parent of four kids. He'll die first.'

"I was sort of not sure that I heard right and I said, 'You said that he will die first?' She got irritated with me at that point and said, 'Yes, that is what I said.' Then she said, 'You will see. You will see. He's a cunt fucker.' I tried to divert her again. I said, 'Tell me her real name. What is her real name? And she said, 'It's Cunt.' That was sort of the end of the first session. Because I couldn't find out what she wanted," Roth added, "I sort of lost control of the whole thing."

Kerry was pleased. This short, prim, middle-aged lady repeating Betty's language and threats had worked well. The jurors looked horrified, exactly the impact she had hoped for. Kerry Wells turned Betty over to Jack Earley.

185

Betty's eyes said it all. Sometimes they were filled with tears. At other times they had the fury of a caged lion. She'd been locked up inside herself for such a long time. Forced to remain silent no matter who was testifying or how they were screwing things up. Finally she'd be allowed to speak.

From the beginning Betty had always believed that once a jury heard what had really happened, they would understand that she had no choice and they'd forgive her. Now sitting on the bench in chains and shackles at five A.M., she was waiting for the trip to court, waiting for her chance to explain, to set the record straight and finally, she hoped, to go home and be with the children.

"Good morning, Mrs. Broderick," Judge Whelan said gently after the clerk swore her in. "Make yourself as comfortable as you can and try to speak into the microphone. We're not in a hurry."

Betty's eyes grew moist. These days a little kindness was all it took to move her to tears. "Thank you," she said. Her voice startled the jury. It was so feminine, so childlike, so incongruous with the obscene language, almost too small for her body. There was a helplessness about it that matched her claims of terror.

Betty began with her childhood, but moved quickly to meeting Dan and falling in love. "We were each other's only intimates on earth," she said, choking back tears. Despite poverty, nine pregnancies, and four live births, she spoke of their happiness as they pursued their dreams. Again Betty talked about Dan in the present tense, as if she had stopped time and kept love alive by killing him.

"Dan's always been very meticulous about his clothes," she said, smiling, "ever since he was a little child. His mother tells stories on him, that he changed his clothes all the time. He loves clothes. He looks very well in clothes. Custom-made lab coats in medical school that no other students had. Double-breasted, fitted, had his initials on them. He was very dapper. Dapper Dan."

Then suddenly she was sobbing, as if those images of the past brought back the the reality of the present.

"Is that something that you were resentful about?" Earley asked after she'd collected herself.

"No," she answered. "It was something that I was proud of."

When asked about her own clothes, she said, "Oh, I didn't need a lot of clothes. I had one cheap long gown that I would wear to hostess. I had my children during the day. No, I didn't spend money on clothes at all."

Earley knew that it was true. Betty hadn't needed fancy clothes then. Christ, she'd barely needed food or sleep. Those were the days when her nourishment seemed to come from giving.

Betty told the jury that as the years passed and Dan was home less and less, she became so lonely and unhappy that she threatened to leave. That's when they attended the marriage encounter weekend.

"Dan told me that he was not the kind of husband or father that he wanted to be. You know," she explained, "he wants to be a very important man. He wants to have a big house and be very prominent and rich. If I would just give him more time, it was really for the children and me that he was doing it. Finally in 1982 we had major money. . . . By 1983 . . . Linda was there. A daily hour-by-hour problem."

With Jack Earley asking questions to guide her, by the end of the day Betty had told the entire story, from burning Dan's clothes to driving through his front door. She had talked about the prisons, the mental institution, the struggle for lawyers and the loss of all four of her children.

The next morning the crowds were larger, the lines longer. Everyone wanted to hear about the killings. People whispered and waited. Even Judge Whelan's face looked alive, intense, and curious.

"The gun was in the center section of my purse," Betty said, "where it had been a long time. The purse was in my car; yes, the purse was in the car all along."

"Did you carry that gun in your purse when the boys were there?" Earley asked.

187

"I always kept it in the purse when the boys were around, yeah. They didn't know it, but I did."

"Why was that?"

"Because it hid very well in that center compartment. I kept the purse with my person. I locked it in the car at night so that they would not be able to find that gun. They had no idea where it was."

"When you went over to Dan's house, it was early in the morning?"

". . . Yes."

"Was there a reason that you went over there so early in the morning?"

"The kids were asleep, Brad was asleep, I went out of the house, it—I just did it. I just thought that I would go talk to him. . . . Just go in, talk to him, and tell him that I couldn't stand it another minute, it was driving me crazy."

"Did you take the gun with you?"

"Yes."

"Why did you take the gun with you?"

"Show of force, a . . . a way to make him listen to me."

"Did you intend to kill yourself?"

"Yes."

"Did you knock on the door, did you ring the doorbell?" Earley asked as he paced back and forth in front of the witness stand.

"No."

"Why not?"

"Because in the past, over the last several five, six years, if I rang the doorbell or something, they would call the police to have me arrested for the restraining order."

"What were you thinking on your way, when you were driving over there?"

". . . I just saw no reason for this to continue. I just had to make it stop, or I was going to kill myself, no problem, I couldn't live like this anymore. . . . I went into the room to talk to them or to wake them up or something. They moved, I moved, and it was over. . . ."

"Real fast."

"I—I hardly really remember being there at all. . . . Dan said something. . . . I grabbed the phone out of the wall and ran out."

"Why did you grab the phone out of the wall and run out?"

"I didn't want him to call the police and have me arrested."

"Are you happy about what you've done," Jack Earley asked.

"Of course not," Betty answered.

Kim was sitting next to Dan's brother Larry, who had flown in from Denver. She was sobbing. Lee was on the other side of the courtroom with Betty's brother from Tennessee. She was also crying.

Outside in the hallway during the recess while spectators, TV crews, and reporters milled around talking and laughing. Lee spotted Kim standing alone near the telephone booths. She walked over and held out her arms. They hugged each other silently.

• 8 •

During cross-examination Kerry Wells attacked hard. She wanted to prove that Betty had been in control, that the obsence language was used deliberately.

"All my life I've never used bad language until recently," Betty told her.

"I'm talking about since February of 1985. Now, you knew that there were appropriate times to use the language, correct?

"Yes, sometimes," Betty answered. "But if I was real nervous or in a state of feeling that I was pressed against the wall. I just started using the language. . . . I was absolutely ranting and screaming. I used it for what it is used for, emphasis."

"You knew there would be times when it would be inappropriate and you wouldn't do it. . . . For example at the divorce trial when you represented yourself, you didn't use any bad or obscene language during the entire trial, correct?"

"I don't remember," Betty answered, looking confused, not realizing herself that she didn't need to use it because she was finally being heard.

Wells jabbed away at every detail. She wanted to know why Betty had never gotten medical attention for her slashed wrists. "Dan was a doctor. He taped them," Betty answered simply.

Kerry asked to see the scars, then announced that there were none. Earley jumped up. "That's improper testimony," he said.

The judge agreed. He ordered the remark stricken from the record, then allowed Betty to show her wrists to the jurors.

Wells kept hammering away, accusing Betty of being evasive and dishonest. She appeared so hard, so ruthless, so totally devoid of sympathy that Earley thought she was losing her edge. "I'm not lying," Betty insisted. "I'm trying to help you and help me to get it right."

Wells kept going relentlessly hour after hour. At side bar, Judge Whelan looked at her and said, "Are you all right?"

"I feel horrible. But it's okay," Wells replied.

"Let's recess," Whelan said.

The next morning she began all over again.

"When you got in the car, did you check your purse to make sure that the gun was in the purse?"

"No."

"Well, you had testified that your plan was to confront Mr. Broderick about the divorce and that if he did not talk to you, that you were going to commit suicide, so obviously you knew that you had to have the gun in order to do that, correct?"

"No," Betty said. "You misspoke the whole thing. There was no plan here. What I'm telling you is that when I read that letter in my kitchen, I gave up on everything."

"I understand, Mrs. Broderick," Kerry said condescendingly.

"I didn't have a plan. I gave up on life. I didn't want to live anymore. Why don't you read what it says on that paper?" Betty said, pointing to the last legal letter she received from Dan's lawyer. "Why don't you read the letter so everyone can see what that letter says, 'that obviously her mental disease and emotional whatever, has not'—it is a horrible letter. They are threatening jail, threatening fines, bullshit, bullshit. At this stage of the game, they are not going to let me speak to my sons. What did Dan and Linda have to gain

190

from putting the answering machine on again, with Linda's voice on it, from not letting me speak to my sons? They were just fucking me over. I couldn't stand it another minute. I had no plan. I died when I read that stuff. I wanted to die. I had no plans. I just wanted to die, just die. That is it. That is the end of the story."

Wells didn't stop. She took Betty through the trip to Dan's house, into the kitchen with the gun in her hand, and up the stairs.

"It was my recollection that the door was closed," Betty said.

"Right," Kerry answered.

"I walked down to where it was open," Betty continued.

"Right. And you knew that was the setup of their house," Kerry interrupted. "You knew there was another door on the other side."

"I knew the bathroom."

"Off the TV room," Kerry said.

"Yes, the bathroom, everything was there. It was a suite," Betty said.

Then suddenly, without further explanation, Kerry Wells, who had never missed a beat, never skipped a detail, never failed to prosecute a single relevant point, jumped past, completely skipped the shooting and the deaths of both Dan and Linda Broderick.

No one in the jury, no one in the press, no one in the spectators' seats, not even Jack Earley, knew why. Perhaps it was misguided legal strategy, or perhaps her own loss, the same loss that had given such passion to her vendetta against Betty Broderick, had also stopped it dead center. Perhaps right at the most critical, dramatic, prosecutorial moment Kerry Wells, who appeared so emotionless, had been done in by her own emotion.

"What happened when you got to the phone booth?" she asked awkwardly after a long pause.

It was not yet clear how badly that omission would hurt her case.

• 9 •

Jack Earley spent another week presenting his defense. First he called Don David Lusterman, a short, dark elegantly dressed family psychologist from Baldwin, New York, who specialized in infidelity.

"When the other person persists in saying the thing is not happening but indeed it is," Lusterman told the jury, "the victim goes into a stage that one of my patients called . . . cold rage. The victim feels crazy. And the infidel will tell the victim that the victim is crazy. . . . There is nothing wrong, you're nuts to be thinking that, et cetera.

"The more a person has been brought up and trained to believe in monogamy and fidelity . . . the more they want to continue believing the truths that they have been taught, the models of marriage that they have seen. . . . Underneath that there is a lot of anxiety . . . brainwashing that goes on when someone is told over and over again that something is not true that is in fact true.

"It makes them lose their sense of reality; it makes them unclear; the cold rage does not explode until the next phase, which is called hot rage, until there is absolutely incontrovertible evidence that is fully accepted by the victim . . . everything that has been pent up, this whole pressure cooker that has been created, begins now to open. It often opens quite violently."

"What happens when people at some point are confronted or come to realize that there is an affair?" Earley asked.

"The person at this point feels utterly and totally betrayed . . . every day is filled with lies, almost everything that you would expect to just accept as gospel truth that is told to you by the infidel suddenly becomes subject to review. . . . That rage often boils inside the person. Frequently such people will become suicidal, filled with despair, feel their whole life has just been turned into a mockery. They barely exist. They either become suicidal or they become very, very ineffectual as parents because they really feel so overwhelmed."

As the afternoon wore on, Lusterman explained that before healing is to begin, certain conditions have to be met. "The infidel has to

192

be able to look at the victim and say, 'I understand that I have deeply hurt you by lying to you, I admit what I have done, and I have remorse for what I have done.' " Betty sat listening with tears streaming down her cheeks as Lusterman continued.

"The next part of the process, which is necessary, is that mourning can occur. But if the infidel absolutely refuses, in effect hands it over to someone and says, 'You take care of this crazy lady,' he is blocking that end of the process. That again is part of the pressure cooker. . . . Healing does not take place, and the feeling of absolute unsupport, confusion, self-hatred, anger toward others tends to persist in the victim."

"Is it common to see statements of bitterness, anger?" Earley asked, trying to bring Lusterman's explanation full circle for the jury.

"Absolutely, absolutely. For example, often a woman will say, 'I could kill myself. How could I have been such a fool? I must be the stupidest person that ever lived.' Or conversely that rage may be expressed toward the other person: 'I'm going to kill that S.O.B.' "

Several of the jurors looked over at Betty. Her eyes were swollen and red. She appeared soft, almost frail, eaten away at.

Earley patted Betty on the shoulder. As if he understood her better now.

Betty's old friends followed. Each gave a short statement. Everything they said supported Lusterman's theories. They all spoke about a smart, funny, loving woman who had become depressed, confused, then violently angry when the structure she had built her life on crumbled.

"Okay," Earley said after Lee's former teacher, Marianne Kunkle, was sworn in, "when you first met Mrs. Broderick, could you describe how she was at that time?"

"Happy, slim, extremely family oriented," Kunkle answered, looking over at Betty. "All for her children. Involved in school class activities. Whatever was needed she would do."

Anne Dick, who was also married to a lawyer and had known Betty for thirteen and a half years, had brought her son to Betty's house to be cared for.

"I could have had anyone that I wanted. . . . But Betty was, in my opinion, the best person . . . she was sort of the consummate mother. If I was to leave Christian with someone, I could not have left him with anyone better than Betty. He was absolutely as happy as he could be being with Betty and Danny."

Candace McCarthy, who met Betty in 1980 and was her Bible-study teacher, added, "I would describe Betty as the personified mother. I mean, if you wanted to find the perfect mother, that beamed around her children, that would be Betty Broderick. She beamed and relished being around her children. I know in the Bible study, after we had broken into groups, we all said a prayer, and she always, I mean, you know, she individually blessed her children and wanted her marriage blessed and her husband blessed."

For two days they filed through nearly twenty of them, people who still loved Betty Broderick because of the way they remembered her.

Of all of them, Lucy Peredun was the most moving. "Mother and child starting over," an ad she had put in the local newspaper said. "Need room in exchange for light housekeeping."

Betty brought extra beds and took her and the little girl in right away. No questions asked. The pain, fear, need, and loneliness were all there in Lucy's eyes.

"There's nothing I want you to do," Betty said. "Forget about the housework. Maria cleans. Just come. Stay as long as you want." They were homeless. They had been battered. Betty fed and sheltered them.

Betty took the child places, bought her clothes and toys. Lucy's daughter loved Betty. "She was like a role model of a mother," Lucy said. "Betty gave me strength to move on in my life. Her love saw me through. If only she could have done the same for herself."

Dr. Daniel Sonkin, an expert on domestic violence and a licensed marriage counselor in Sausalito, California, tried to explain why Betty couldn't be as kind to herself as she'd been to Lucy.

"My opinion," Sonkin told the jury, "is that Mr. Broderick physically, sexually, and psychologically abused Mrs. Broderick. . . . Battered women just don't broadcast this information, and men don't broadcast this to their friends, so one of the difficulties in these types of cases is to try to look for certain patterns. On numerous occasions

194

he came home intoxicated, on numerous occasions he forced her to have sex; he would get angry and break things. He was very psychologically abusive to her. The first incidence of physical violence happened while they were dating. Although Mrs. Broderick believed that it wasn't a serious problem or that it would go away, it just got worse over time."

Kerry Wells didn't like this. Again and again she tried to discredit Sonkin. Attacked everything from the fact that he held a doctorate but was not an M.D. to his concept of abuse.

The next day she produced a string of rebuttal witnesses. One of Dan's housekeepers said that he had dinner with the children every night. Another claimed she never saw him have more than one or two glasses of wine a month. The final rebuttal witness, Dr. Melvin Goldzband, said that no increase in alimony, no custody arrangements, no property settlement would have satisfied Betty. "She wanted Dan. She wanted not to be rejected." Goldzband, who was a forensic psychiatrist, suggested that she was not out of control but suffered from a mixed personality disorder and was severely narcissistic.

Then Earley called his rebuttal expert, psychologist Kay Di Francesca. "Her use of language was so explosive," Di Francesca said, "that it constantly worked against her. It ended up her getting fined and vilified, with people talking about her . . . and going to jail. Really, it just shows how out of control she was. This is not what a nice girl educated and trained like Mrs. Broderick does."

Kerry Wells stood up to cut her off.

"I'm not finished," Di Francesca said. "The failure of empathy with her children is really interesting because it really relates to the lack of power that this woman feels . . . she really does not recognize the effect that she has on other people. In fact she thinks that she has no effect. She certainly does not recognize that what she was saying hurt her children. She thought that, 'Oh, no, they know me, they know that I don't mean it.' "

Di Francesca said finally that Betty's obscene messages, her acts of vandalism, and the shootings were not thought out or planned. They were exactly the opposite, the result of a spontaneous loss of the "executive function to control emotions."

195

When it was time for Kerry Wells to make her closing argument, the gravity and intensity of her manner made it clear that she did not intend to lose her first murder trial.

Calling it an ambush and a double execution, she argued that Betty knew exactly what she was doing. "You do not point a thirty-eight-caliber gun loaded with hollow-point bullets at two people lying in a bed only inches away, early in the morning, and fire without intending to kill them. Betty Broderick's claim that she wanted to confront her ex-husband is hogwash, absolutely hogwash," she said. "There was no way she truly expected Daniel Broderick to talk to her about the divorce after being confronted at five-thirty or six in the morning in his bedroom."

Wells paused and looked down at her notes. Her eyes swept the jurors. She walked closer.

"There was also no way that Betty Broderick contemplated suicide. If she did that," Wells added, "then clearly Dan and Linda would have won, since Betty Broderick knew that's what they wanted. If she wanted to confront him, why, before she fired, didn't she say, 'Hold it, I want to talk to you'? Why wasn't there a confrontation if she wanted a confrontation. The law does not allow a person to charge into other people's homes with a loaded gun, to confront them, catch them totally off guard, unprotected, helpless, and kill them both, and then say, 'But gosh, I didn't really mean it. I shouldn't be responsible.' She's responsible for murder, period."

She was at the mercy of her emotions, out of control, like a boat without a rudder, Jack Earley argued when his turn came. Her act was one of craziness, one of emotion, one that should never have happened. It was Daniel Broderick, not Betty, who embarked on a campaign—a plan of "crazy-making behavior"—that left Betty in the throes of emotions. Betty Broderick admits firing the fatal shots. But there was no premeditation and deliberation in this case. This was not the act of someone who wants to be the princess and the victim."

For four days the jury argued. Then, at 3:52 on November 20, the foreman, twenty-six-year-old Lucenda Swann, handed Judge Whelan a note that said they could not agree on a verdict of either manslaughter or murder. They were hopelessly deadlocked. "We do not feel" the note added, "that further deliberations on the evidence would change that decision." Most of them left silently, but when nineteen-year-old Nicole Prentice was stopped by a reporter, she said, "We understood both sides of the case, but we could not find agreement."

Sixty-two-year old David Southwick added, "I'm going to say one thing, and that's all I'm going to say: No, it wasn't even close."

• 10 •

With ninety percent of herself Kerry Wells really didn't want to do it again, but there was a part of her that couldn't stop. This was unfinished business. It just wasn't complete. She would have felt that she had given up, and that feeling of defeat would have stayed with her for the rest of her life.

Getting ready for the trial all over again was really bad, much worse than the first time. She had to live with all the criticism about how she had lost the first trial.

Kerry wanted an assistant to take some of the pressure off. She asked for Paul Burakoff, a fraud specialist she'd worked with before. Burakoff, a tall, thin, gray-haired attorney, agreed and provided some relief. Back at the office the Domestic Violence Unit was just getting started. Even with Burakoff's help, Wells couldn't give either job her full attention.

Jack Earley was having his own struggles. As a private attorney doing murder cases, he earned $250 an hour. The costs of Betty's first trial totaled half a million. Between that and her divorce she was now broke. The $300,000 in equity on the house that Wolf sold was completely gone. She had deeded over her condominium to Brad, so he couldn't touch that. People were calling Earley's office with donations for the new trial, but they didn't amount to much. If Betty was found indigent, which she certainly would be after the county Department of Revenue and Recovery reviewed her case, Earley would be lucky to get $60 or $65 an hour. Still, it was unfinished business for him too. He was getting an enormous amount of press attention, and it was great for his career.

Finally at Betty's request Earley decided to stay on with the case and petition the court for additional payment. Within a week all of the same players, even Judge Whelan, were back in the courthouse getting ready to do it all over again.

Earley was arguing for bail. "She's an evil monster in a harmless-looking package," Dan's brother Larry protested. "If this woman is released on bail and shows up in Colorado, I fear, we fear, and the court should probably assume that there will be bloodshed." Larry, who had temporary custody of Danny and Rhett, added, "Any contact with Betty would be a disaster for the children."

Whelan took it under advisement. "I have to consider the protection of the public." he announced a week later. "I'm aware that the defendant is accused of having committed two violent crimes and that she's admitted to having killed two people. I'm aware that at one time the defendant freely carried a firearm and that she still faces the possibility of life in prison without parole, thus I find that a continuance of her no-bail status is fully justified."

• 11 •

All Betty wanted was to see the boys, to lay her eyes on them and kiss them one more time. They had been whisked away to Larry Broderick's house in Colorado, right after Dan and Linda died.

Betty hadn't been allowed to see them, speak to them, or write to them since that morning almost two years ago when she'd left them still asleep in their beds.

198

Twice the judge had said no when Betty begged to send them cards on their birthdays and at Christmas.

Larry Broderick and the Gray Cary, Ames and Frye legal firm were still trying to stop her from seeing them. Finally Betty was granted a meeting with Child Protective Services. They set the rules. She couldn't say a word about Dan. She couldn't say a word about Linda. She couldn't say a word about jail. She couldn't talk about this, and she couldn't talk about that. But they approved a visit in the judge's chambers at the downtown divorce court on Sixth Avenue.

Oh, my God, Betty kept thinking. *I'm going to say the wrong thing. It's going to be awkward. I'm going to cry.* Then Betty walked in the door and saw them standing there. It was like a miracle. Her sons, her boys, so handsome, so beautiful, standing right there. It felt like it had been forever. At the same time it was as if they hadn't been apart for one minute.

Rhett jumped onto her lap and threw his arms around her neck. He hugged her and kissed her over and over again. That's where he stayed, right on her lap, the whole visit. Everyone was laughing and talking and kissing and hugging all at once.

Betty had always been a pretender, always acted with the kids as if everything was going to be just fine. So today she just kept right on pretending that she was handling it all. She made jokes so that they wouldn't be sad and feel sorry for her. She didn't want to upset them.

She thought it was very important that she keep it light, just as she did whenever Kim and Lee visited her in prison. They'd bring their friends, and Betty would tell jokes. She'd make jewelry out of straw from the broom and use little pieces of tin foil to make diamond studs. She'd glue them on with toothpaste. She'd have them all in hysterics because she didn't want the kids' friends to say, "Oh, your poor mother's in jail."

Sometimes Betty thought it was a disservice, that talent of hers, because even when she was in the depths of depression, even when she couldn't breathe, she'd click in, she'd entertain them, she'd be perfect. She could pull it together because she had that hide-your-feelings, the-show-must-go-on upbringing. She had always been the perfect hostess. She had always pretended to the kids that everything was going to be fine, just fine.

Even now, even today, if she didn't look into Rhett's sad eyes or really see Danny's beautiful square jaw, or touch their fingers with hers, if she didn't stop long enough to feel the suffering she had caused them, she could still do it.

Danny brought yellow roses. Rhett brought perfume. They both brought pictures to share. Betty had presents for them too. Presents that were totally illegal. An entire bottle of green shampoo, which she'd hidden in the big pocket of her brown prison suit, and candy kisses and Tootsie Rolls that she'd been saving up for weeks.

They hadn't bothered to search her that morning, and when the prison marshall saw the stuff, she said, "Oh, my God, Betty, you know you're not allowed to give them any presents." But even she didn't have the heart to keep the kids from taking the stuff.

The girls had come too. They didn't want to miss it. So all four kids just kept talking to her at once. She forgot whether it was an hour or two hours, but it seemed like five minutes. The shortest, the longest, the most precious five minutes of her life, because all four of her children still wanted her.

It was the one fleeting hour that she would relive every night when she closed her eyes and put her head down on that prison cot. Every night the laughter, the excitement, and the joy came floating back. Every night she'd try to slip into the unconsciousness of sleep before the marshal returned and took the children away. Before the pain and the loss came crashing back.

• 12 •

Betty Broderick on Brad Today

"I never expected Brad would stay through trials or visit me in jail. I told him at the beginning, I said, 'Thank you for everything you've been to me.' My thank-you note said, 'Thank you so much. We have had so much fun. You've been such a nice person. But forget about me. Go and be free now. Go on with your life. You tried, you really tried to make things better. You tried to make me happy, but it had nothing to do with you. You couldn't get me my children back and make things right.'

"I was never emotionally available to love Brad. After my husband did such a job on me, no matter how wonderful, how rich, or how handsome Brad was, I couldn't love him. Love to me is total trust and total knowing. That's what love is to me. It is total commitment.

"Brad never said, 'I'll support you and the kids.' He doesn't want the responsibility. I didn't look to him as the next step. But when he stuck with me through the trials, I began to hope. I said, 'Danny needs a home. Rhett needs a home. You could be a father to them.' Brad didn't want that. In some ways he's still like a child himself. He became the substitute child for the children I had lost. I made no demands on him. He never made any on me.

"Still, Brad has made some type of bond, some type of real, strong, important connection with me and my children.

"Sometimes I still think we could get married now. He could come up here on these five-day family visits that they have, where you stay in a cottage together. He could bring the boys here. If he's not immediate family, he can't stay.

"My condo is directly across the street from restaurants and movie theaters. Danny and Rhett could be independent if they lived with him. Brad is in my condo living alone. He'd never be living like that. He lived in a little tiny, tiny rental house down at the beach because he didn't want any responsibility. In his own way Brad is still there for us. All of my friends call him. He takes care of my outside life and things for me. And I'll always be grateful, very, very grateful. But it's sad, you know, because Brad's in my house with all my beautiful things and I still have two little boys who need a daddy and a home."

• 13 •

Jack Earley had a lot to do before he got back to Betty's case. A federal trial that would take about four weeks and at least two other smaller murder trials. As if that wasn't enough, Earley's house caught on fire. The witness list, phone numbers, and transcripts all got burned. One short in the VCR ended up costing over three hundred thousand dollars in damages. Then there was the cancer on his lip that required surgery. That pushed Betty's trial all the way to September.

Betty found waiting so hard that she put on the cheerful, upbeat routine to cover her anxiety. Her back ached constantly.

"It's like a country club in here," she said, smiling. "I don't mind waiting for the trial at all. You walk around. There's no stress, no responsibility. I don't even have to worry about getting my car fixed. I can read, I can converse with people. I can write. I even love it in lockdown. It's bigger and it's quieter. I can exercise." They believed her.

"She's having too much fun. Who the hell does the rich bitch think she is, Thelma and Louise or something?" one of the guards mumbled. Books were being written, films were being made, now ABC was coming to interview her for *20/20.*

Since she liked isolation so much, they'd put her back. Seven of them showed up in her cell one night two weeks before the trial. One was carrying a video camera. They said she'd committed an infraction earlier in the week.

Really it was another prisoner who'd pushed her to the ground and taunted her when they were chained together on a bench. When Betty screamed and tried to defend herself. The guards warned she'd be punished.

Now when she saw them coming with the video camera, she jumped onto the top bunk. She was only wearing a sweatshirt and green underpants. "No pictures, no videos, please." They told her she was going to solitary, and they started pulling. She held on to the bed and began kicking.

One of the guards got kicked in the chest and hit her head against the bracket that held the bed against the cell wall. "Let me go," Betty yelled. Another guard grabbed her.

Then all of them, except for the one with the video camera, picked her up and carried her screaming into an isolation cell. The following morning it was all over the news.

"Elizabeth Broderick may have given prosecutors another tool in her upcoming double murder trial," the *Union* wrote, "by injuring three sheriff's deputies in a brief jailhouse scuffle."

"If anything happened to those deputies," Betty said, "they broke a fingernail trying to stick it into me."

"Betty goes on a rampage, injures three," the *San Diego Tribune* reported.

Actually Betty was more embarrassed by the way she looked when she saw the video than by anything else. "If you'd been locked up in a teeny-tiny room for two years, you'd have flabby thighs too," she said.

Wells was trying to get a gag order. Whelan denied the request.

Sheriff Captain Nelda Spencer announced that the video had been made as a matter of policy, to lessen the risk of liability for the sheriff's department, because the use of force was considered a possibility.

Four days later one of the guards, Michelle St. Clair, announced that she had suffered a strained shoulder and would be suing Betty for her injuries. Then her lawyer, James Cunningham, called a press conference and released his edited version of the tape to TV stations. It was on every nightly news station. Pretty soon the late-night shows were also grabbing for it.

When ABC's Tom Jarriel showed up, she was allowed out of her isolation cell to talk briefly to him. That interview was later aired on Barbara Walters's *20/20.* So was the video.

"The whole thing was a setup," Betty told reporters, "to keep me from getting a good jury just two weeks before my trial. It's bogus rhetoric. They still believe I'm rich, so they're suing me. I wasn't prepared. It was seven against one. Hell, I wasn't even dressed. Think about it. How could I fight against and injure seven armed and ready guards?"

• 14 •

Kerry Wells had changed her approach. As heavily as she had avoided Dan and Linda's death in the first trial, she focused on them this time. Betty saw the pictures out of the corner of her eye. A big courtroom display. Linda was on the left side of the bed, all bloody. "Oh, no, Jack, that's not how it was," Betty whispered. "Linda wasn't on that side of the bed. Linda was on this side of the bed, and Dan was over there. They have the models in the wrong places."

"Those aren't the models, Betty, those are Dan and Linda," Jack said.

"Oh, God," Betty moaned. "I had no idea, none. I never saw what the room looked like until just now."

Then, to Betty's surprise, Jack brought in a bed, a real full-sized bed covered with a blood-soaked handmade blue cross-stitched quilt. "That was my quilt," Betty whispered, "the one I bought in Amish Country in Ohio. I never saw it. I didn't even know that Dan had taken that quilt. I never thought about it. I haven't seen it in years, ever since we moved out of the Coral Reef house."

Pictures of the armoire over where the phone was came next. Betty had pulled out the phone so that Dan couldn't call the cops, but she had never seen the armoire. That was the whole point of the gun in the first place. Then there was a picture of Dan lying on the floor. Suddenly, as if Dan's death was real to her now, Betty was crying. "Oh, God," she said to Jack with tears streaming down her face. "I thought the little fucker was still after me. That's why I acted like that. I swear to God. I have no clear recollection of any of this."

• 15 •

The new tactic was really getting to Betty. Dan and Linda were alive again and being killed very slowly. Kerry Wells hoped it would hit the new jury just as hard. Unlike the first jury these were mostly blue-collar workers, electricians, technicians, mechanics, and several very young women. There was only one middle-aged woman in the entire group, a former telephone operator, and even she had never been divorced. Betty wouldn't get much sympathy here.

In an effort to keep up with Wells, who was using more props, including a videotape of Dan and Linda's house and the route Betty took the morning of the shootings, Earley also tried a new, dramatic approach. He brought out a photograph of the Broderick family in a frame and then he smashed it. "Glass didn't protect a family," he shouted at the jury. "It was shattered, and Elizabeth Broderick tried to hold the picture together." Two reporters in the press section rolled their eyes.

Kerry Wells's attempt to maximize the horror of the deaths continued. Dr. Christopher Swalwell, a pathologist, had changed his testimony. For the first time he said he believed that Dan's wound had only broken the skin of the chest wall. "It was not," in his opinion, "a through-and-through wound, and Dan Broderick could probably have survived if he had gotten medical attention."

Then two ghostlike foam dummies of Dan and Linda were brought into the courtroom. They were pierced with dowels to show the paths of the bullets. Wells left them lying there propped up naked against the wall day after day, just to remind the jury of the victims.

Next Maria Peralta, a new witness for the prosecution, took the stand. Peralta didn't have the best credentials, but Wells hoped she could help establish premeditation and lack of remorse. "I'm a working girl. I was in jail for prostitution and heroin addiction," Peralta said. "Betty said to me, 'Linda has been in my bed for seven years. . . . I had five bullets. I only got three in.' She never said she was sorry for anything."

"Were you paid for your testimony?" Earley asked. Peralta smiled seductively. "Being a working girl," she answered, "I never do something for nothing."

Jack Earley's first day to present the defense was Halloween. The court stenographer showed up wearing orange socks and pumpkin earrings.

Earley brought in the bloody sheets and spread them out on the makeshift double bed. Someone joked that the ghosts of Dan and Linda would arrive any minute. Betty cried at the defense table. Earley was trying to prove that Dan and Linda were awake and moving around when Betty fired. He kept pointing at the pattern of blood on the sheets. Wells jumped right in to help. She picked up the models of Dan and Linda and put them on the bed.

"It was risky," Jack Earley acknowledged after he saw some of the jurors' expressions, "but I was trying to show that there was a lot of movement."

When Betty took the stand the next morning, the rest of Kerry Wells's new strategy became clear. If Betty's eyes filled with tears, Wells said, "Let's take a break." If Earley asked a question that might elicit an emotional or sympathetic response, Wells objected. Betty could hardly get a word out without being interrupted.

During cross-examination Wells pounded away relentlessly and accused Betty of lying. "I wish Dan was here to tell you the truth," Betty said, crying.

"I wish he was here too," Wells snapped.

"Oh, so do I," Betty said again, sobbing.

"You saw Dan and Linda on the bed," Wells persisted after they took a break.

"I have no recollection of seeing them at all," Betty answered.

"How do you know they moved if you didn't see them?" she asked. Betty looked confused.

"I know now who was where, and I know that I had the impression then that she was closest to me, but . . ."

"It was your testimony," Kerry Wells reminded Betty as she marched before the witness stand, "that when you entered the room, Linda moved toward Dan. Linda yelled, 'Call the police,' and Dan moved toward the phone. Did you see any of that happen?"

Betty paused. Her eyes narrowed. "That's the impression of the whole thing that I have," she whispered.

"So you saw that happen. Correct?" Wells pressed.

"I don't remember seeing Linda or Dan at all. It was just blurs," Betty answered.

"What frightened you?" Wells asked.

"I entered about to say something. They said something first. They started to move, and I just panicked. It was not a thought process. I moved, they moved, the gun went off, and it was over that fast."

"You pulled the trigger," Kerry Wells said, her voice deepening with intensity. "That was a voluntary act on your part, right?"

"I don't remember pulling the trigger," Betty answered. "No, I was totally in an altered state of consciousness. I already testified I didn't even remember driving there. I was scared to death of confronting Dan Broderick, which I always was because he scared me. . . . I moved, they moved, the gun went off. I just tensed like that." Betty extended her arms to demonstrate.

"You testified that if the confrontation didn't work, you were going to kill yourself," Wells continued, staring into Betty's eyes. "But the gun never came up to your head. It went into their bodies, didn't it?"

"It was like a reflex action," Betty repeated, almost pleadingly. She started to say, "Don't you understand, I always loved Dan Broderick, I was living in terror. I was close to collapse." But Kerry Wells silenced her. *That's enough*, Wells's eyes seemed to say. *You've given me what I wanted. It's done. You're finished.*

• 16 •

Jack Earley had a hot new lead. He walked toward Betty. "Did Dan ever discuss having you killed?" he asked without warning.

Betty's face turned pale. Her mouth dropped open, and she began to cry. Earley looked over at the press and the jury. The corners of his mouth turned up. He was pleased to see the impact that Betty's unrehearsed response was having. "Certainly not," she managed.

Wells jumped up. "Objection," she shouted.

"Ignore that remark," the judge told the jury. He ordered it stricken from the record.

"If I can go a little farther, Your Honor," Earley said, "we have Paul Taylor, whom Mr. Broderick solicited for the murder of—"

Wells jumped up again. "That's not correct, Your Honor," she said, visibly shaken.

"Your statement is incorrect," Whelan echoed, glaring at Earley. "You're posturing for the benefit of reporters in the courtroom. Knock it off."

"I am not, Your Honor," Earley answered, his own voice rising.

Wells sprang up out of her seat for the third time. "That's not fair, Judge," she yelled, throwing her notebooks on the table. Then her voice rose wildly. "Do something about it."

"Clear the courtroom," Whelan shouted.

That was it. Whelan imposed a gag order forbidding Earley or Wells to talk to the press. The next day no one was allowed in the courtroom. Not the press nor the jury nor the spectators.

When Whelan announced that afternoon that both the hearings and the transcripts of the morning's closed discussions would be kept from the press, an attorney for the *San Diego Union and Tribune* protested. Reporters followed him into the closed courtroom. "This violates the right to freedom of the press. It is abuse of judicial discretion," the attorney said.

"Granting public access to evidence in a hearing to determine whether that evidence is admissible in court would undermine the right to a fair trial," Whelan answered, taking the attorney on. Once again he ordered reporters out of the courtroom.

Gag orders and sealed courtrooms were nothing new to Betty. The marshal wrapped the chains around her waist and snapped the hand-cuffs onto both her wrists. "This is just how Dan always did it," she whispered to Jack Earley. "Everything sealed. It's like he's still here."

"I've never seen her all chained up before," one of the reporters said softly. Betty overheard and smiled sadly. Then, as if she didn't want anyone, even the press, to feel sorry for her, she did a little pirouette and began turning her body as if the waist chains were some new designer belt she was modeling at Saks.

• 17 •

The next day it started all over again. Wells and her coprosecutor Burakoff requested that the courtroom be cleared while the attorneys argued about the alleged hit man. Paul Taylor, a cab driver, had called Jack Earley and claimed that Daniel Broderick said, "How much would it cost me to get my wife killed?" Whelan's exterior manner was still calm, but his direction was becoming clearer. Because Betty admitted she didn't know about the alleged hit man, Whelan concluded that it could not have affected her state of mind. Therefore, he said, the testimony was irrelevant.

The next issue was Daniel Sonkin. Kerry Wells did not want him up there this time telling the jury, as he had in the last trial, that Betty was a battered wife. There was no doubt about it. It would be very damaging to her case to have the jury told that Betty had been physically, sexually, and psychologically abused over a period of sixteen years.

Finally Sonkin told reporters waiting in the hallway outside the sealed courtroom that his testimony had been limited so much that there was no point in taking the stand. "I interviewed her for thirteen hours face-to-face," he said. "She was given the battered-woman's questionnaire. I also interviewed Lee; and her parents; and her brother, Frank; and her sister, Claire; and several of her friends. Kerry Wells knows exactly what I found.

"Betty initially denied being an abused woman," Sonkin said, "but as the interview went on, she was sad and tearful and she began to recall with greater clarity specifics of the abuse. Like many victims of spousal abuse, she experienced shame and humiliation at admitting her victimization, and she tends to minimize the impact that it had on her. But there was all kinds of evidence. It was very intimidating, very degrading . . . the battering and the way he abused her contributed to her deterioration."

"No way," Sonkin continued, "was I going to take the stand after they had gone through every single question that Mr. Earley was going to ask and told me that nine tenths of them were irrelevant.

"It is a process I have never before experienced in the twelve years I've been doing expert testimony. From thirty-seven pages of testimony that I gave during the last trial they cut me down to two. That's what they ruled in there.

"Dan Broderick was trying to wear her down. He was continuing to abuse her. He was pushing her to the edge. But they wouldn't let me say any of it. The defense will rest its case tomorrow," he said. "And the jury will never know what really happened. You people know. It's just a shame that the jurors, the people who need to know, won't."

• 18 •

Betty Broderick on Love

"Dan was my heart and soul. I couldn't see myself actually being with anyone else. I was so traumatized by this whole thing that I never wanted to trust and love that much again, because I couldn't be hurt that much again. So to protect myself I would never give myself away again so totally.

"Maybe, if I had ever remarried, I would have had a lot more of what people now call a modern-day marriage. I think that's true with everyone who remarries. Once you break the original bond that you swore in front of God and everyone that you'd never break, once you break that, the subsequent ones will mean nothing.

"The first time I went to a wedding, I cried because I was thinking, *How can that man stand there and look his lovely second bride in the eyes and promise her the same things he promised to someone else and didn't keep? What's going to make him keep it with her? What's going to make her any different? Nothing.* Once the original bond is broken, then who cares? Five, six marriages until it doesn't work anymore. And the definition of 'doesn't work' can be as simple as 'I don't feel like it.' It doesn't have to be anything meaningful. 'I'm not in the mood. Let's get married until I'm not in the mood anymore.'

"There's also something about the very early connection, like the one I had with Dan, that I could never get over. We were not a first generation. I like to see myself in perspective of civilization. This was the way couples and families have been with marriage. There is supposed to be no adultery and no divorce as far back as biblical times. It was breaking the rules back then. We've come all this way in many areas like science and medicine, but it's still breaking the rules.

"Life is too short. You cannot make several families. It screws

211

everyone up. It screws the kids up, it screws the men up, it screws the grandchildren up, you've broken the chain of family. Everyone connected directly to this chain suffers. So I was saying, 'Never again for me, never will I be open to what I was open to when I believed in Dan and married him.'

"That's the way I wanted to raise my daughters, to find real, committed love and work through problems together. I think that really is the meaning of life instead of in and out of relationships all the time. It worked for me and it worked for Dan, too, for a long time. We really were the perfect couple. And still I miss him so much. I think it was the new money that turned his head. You know that Bee Gees' song, 'How could a love so right turn out so wrong?' That's how it was for us.

"I had no reservations in my marriage. I left no part of myself on reserve in case it didn't work out. I was in it heart and soul and both feet. 'Forsaking all others till death do us part.' "

• 19 •

Theresa Cinti had just put the baby down for a nap. She flipped on Court TV. The camera was holding on Betty. "Oh, my God," Theresa said, "that's her. That's the lady we saw in Harrah's Casino. The one whose husband wanted to kill her."

Suddenly the whole thing came flooding back. It was 1983. She and her boyfriend, Charles Smith, were at Harrah's for the weekend. Charles had been gambling, losing money. He sat down at the bar and ordered a soda. He never drank when he gambled. An immaculately dressed man with a starched shirt and a flower in his lapel came over and sat down next to him.

"How are you doing?" the man said.

"I'm losing," Charles answered. "I'm afraid I'll never be able to dress like you."

"What do you do for a living?" the man asked.

"It's my last year of college," Charles said. "I'm a reserve police officer, but I'm starting law school in the fall."

"I'm a lawyer," the man said. "Are you married?"

"Not yet," Charles answered.

"Well, don't."

Smith thought it was a joke, one of those things people say in bars. But the man kept drinking and talking. He said he hated his wife and was going to have her killed or push her over the brink and drive her crazy. He said he was going to take the kids away from her. He said something about getting access to a gun and that it would be easy to do away with her.

Smith looked at him. It wasn't the kind of conversation you had with your best friend, much less with a stranger sitting next to you at a bar. The guy didn't sound drunk, but this was like something you'd see in a movie where people overhear other people talking about killing someone. It was so horrifying that Smith could feel his own eyes bulging out of his head.

Smith had been a reserve cop for years. He was used to dealing with criminals. But this seemed different. Something about this guy scared him when the man began to say something about hiring a hit man and making it worth his while. Smith panicked. He absolutely freaked out.

"I've got to go find my girlfriend," he stammered.

Terry was playing slots. He grabbed her and took her over to the side. He was shaking, actually gasping for air. "What's wrong? What happened to you?" she said. She'd been dating the guy for almost three years and had never seen him look like this before.

"You'll never believe the conversation I just had," he whispered. He began to tell her.

At first Terry wasn't interested. She figured it was just another divorce. But when he got to the part about having his wife killed and looking for a hit man, she said, "Where is this guy?" They climbed a couple of stairs to get a better view across the crowded room.

"He's right over there," Smith said, pointing as the man walked over to an exit near the bar.

"We've got to tell the cops," Terry said.

"No," Smith answered. "We can't. We have no proof."

"It's intent to kill," she told him. "You're always telling me about intent to kill. Let's call the cops and tell them you met a guy who has an intent to kill."

"No," Smith repeated. "We're not going to do that."

As they talked, they could see a woman walk over to the man. A tall blonde wearing a gold or metallic dress, a knockout, a fancy dresser just like the man.

"I'm going over there to warn her," Theresa said. "I'm going to tell her."

Smith held onto her arm. "No, stay out of it," he said.

"Let go of me," Theresa insisted.

"No," Smith answered, raising his voice and holding her arm tighter. "You stay out of this."

The man looked over and saw them on the stairs gesturing and arguing. For the first time in their relationship Theresa hit Smith. She broke away and started pushing frantically through the crowd toward the man and the woman. She was inches away. The man was staring her down.

He knows I know, Theresa thought. The man turned and led the woman through a set of doors. The doors closed behind them. Charles Smith pushed through the crowd and caught up with Theresa.

"They're gone," he said. "We lost them."

"It was no accident that he told you all that," Theresa said. "He saw your gun when you took it out to give it to the security guard. You stood there holding it in your hand making a spectacle of yourself for about fifteen minutes. I bet he wanted to proposition you. We've got to go to the cops."

"I told you, we're not going," Smith insisted. "Just forget it. We'll never find them. There's no way for you to open those doors. They have no handles, they're electronically controlled. There's a show going on in there."

"Then I'll wait here," Theresa said. "If they went into that room, they've got to come out."

"There's probably another exit." Smith laughed. "Look, this is not your responsibility."

"Dammit," she said. "What if he kills her?"

They fought about it all night. She tried to leave. Smith took her wallet.

"Cut it out," he said. "I love you, I want to marry you."

The next morning they turned on the news. When no murder was reported, Smith said, "See, I told you, you overreacted."

"Just wait," she answered. "This will come back to haunt us."

Now Theresa picked up the phone. She called Jack Earley's office and told him everything. Earley called Charles Smith, who had finished law school and was now an assistant D.A. himself, over in San Mateo County. "Of course I remember the incident," he said. "It changed my life. Theresa and I broke up over it. I'm married to someone else now, and so is she. We were never able to repair the damage of that night. It was the strangest, most surreal encounter of my entire life. Yes of course I'll come to San Diego with her and testify if you need me."

A few hours later Jack Earley called back. "I'm sorry," he said. "Maybe someday, based on this, we'll be able to get Betty a new trial, but for now the judge won't let you testify. We're already in the rebuttal phase. We've missed our chance."

• 20 •

The afternoon before his closing argument Jack Earley had an idea. He rushed out to a hardware store and bought a metronome. "Everyone has a point where things happen to them," he said as he started up the metronome. It droned back and forth. "This is not a case where we are telling you that Elizabeth Broderick has no responsibility. It's like looking at a pipe, like rust that slowly starts eating

215

through. . . . It's like listening to this thing here," Earley pointed to the metronome and tried to explain what he wanted it to symbolize. "The first tick, the second tick, the sound isn't enough to drive you crazy, but after you hear it over and over . . . " His voice trailed as he shut the metronome off, never finishing his thought.

No one looked impressed, but Jack Earley didn't seem to notice. He spoke for another four hours, sometimes effectively, sometimes rambling. "When she's feeling pain and rage, when her trust has been ripped apart," Earley said in one of his better moments, "Dan Broderick doesn't say, 'I'm sorry,' he says, 'You're crazy. All the kids know Mom's crazy.' 'She's crazy, she's just crazy'—that's what Kim hears. Then he calls her up and says, 'It was twenty years ago today,' then he sends her flowers and says, 'I hope you're feeling better,' like it's a sickness that he had nothing to do with."

After that Earley wandered through a replay of the entire trial. But instead of moving forward chronologically he seemed to jump from thought to thought.

There were some good lines, some points well made, but sometimes the repertoire became a harangue that failed to separate the important from the trivial. Betty shifted in her seat, looking uncomfortable. The jurors grew restless. Earley kept right on going until he had practically lost his voice, apparently giving no thought to time.

"There was a loophole," he whispered hoarsely. "Linda was the wife. They put her back on. They knew this upset her." A series of fragmented half-formed ideas followed. "She still won't talk nice about Dan Broderick," Earley said. "There are problems, there is a lack of empathy. She was lonely. She didn't have anything left. She was trying to get back on track. The answering machine with Linda starts, the fines start. The letter arrives saying her mental disease has not improved. . . . You didn't see any of that in the summer when she had the children. It's like getting a wound and having it reopened. It hurts more when its reopened. There are things you miss when they no longer get dressed up for Halloween or ride a tricycle." Exhausted, Jack Earley seemed to be winding up.

"She went in there to confront Dan," he said. "She did what she had done before when things had gotten bad. She went over to confront Dan. She went to the first open door. She said, 'All I remember is opening the door and stepping in.' They move. She fires the gun.

"Now," Earley whispered, gesturing now toward the jurors, because his voice was almost gone, "you will have to decide: In that split second was there an intent to kill? Did she premeditate and deliberate, and it's obvious she did not.

"Is there an intent to kill?" he asked again. "I think you have to look at the case, look at all the evidence, not just one piece. That's what the law tells you to do. I think if you do all that, if you understand, there is no doubt, there is no premeditation or deliberation. She was at her daughter's house, sick. She didn't know what was going on. I think you will see there is no premeditation. She should be held responsible," Early concluded, "but it should be linked to her mental state. Thank you."

• 21 •

This was the culmination of the case that Kerry Wells had been planning and rehearsing since the end of the first trial. She corrected every omission and fixed every error. Not a word was wasted or unrehearsed or without a purpose.

Wells trembled like an actress on opening night as she thanked the jury for being there and told them how important their job was. Something in the intensity in her voice seemed to say, *This is for Dan Broderick, this is for Linda Broderick, this is for my murdered friend, this is for my father.*

"Elizabeth Broderick took a loaded gun," she told the jury, "and blew two people away in their sleep. People always have reasons for what they do," Wells added to minimize Earley's main point. "It's a given that people have reasons, and we have a compassionate system, but that doesn't mean that we don't demand that people remain legally responsible for their actions. No matter how you may feel about Elizabeth Broderick, the fact of the matter is she made the judgment. She is the one who chose not to build herself up but to tear Dan and Linda down.

"People have a right to make choices, but they are responsible. . . . There is no question that Betty Broderick killed Dan and Linda with expressed malice. . . . No one but Elizabeth Broderick pulled that trigger again and again and again and again.

"The cold, hard facts of what happened in that room are indisputable. The fact is there is no getting around that the gun was pointed at Linda's heart. There is no question that she had to change her position to shoot Dan in the bed. There is no getting around the fact that she had to change her aim again to shoot the back of Linda's head. Was it panic shooting?" Kerry Wells asked. "No, it was good shooting," she said, answering her own question.

"The defendant says 'I just barely entered the room and Linda immediately yelled, "Call the police." Dan moved and I flinched and shot.' . . . How does that excuse her conduct? 'It's not my fault,' she seems to be saying, 'I shot them because they yelled.' What did they do? They moved away. Even assuming the truth of her testimony, they tried to get away and she shot them in the back. That is murder.

"Think about it. She knew Dan wasn't going to talk to her under those circumstances at five-thirty in the morning in bed with his wife. This woman knows how to confront when she wants to. She said she bought the gun for a show of force. Why didn't she use it for a show of force then?

"If there is some remaining speck of doubt in your mind," she said with quiet intensity, "then it has got to disappear when you think of what she did afterward. She knew she had fired the gun and she knew she had fired it at them. She saw Dan roll out of the bed. She saw Linda motionless. She didn't say, 'Oh, my God.' . . . She pulled the phone out of the wall so he couldn't call for help.

"This is not panic conduct. It is incredibly cold-blooded, calculated conduct. It is acting with express knowledge. It's actually hard to imagine anyone acting with more malice. The fact is," Kerry Wells said without missing a beat. "They were in their own house minding their own business, sleeping in their own beds. The law does not allow people to do this and then say, I really didn't mean to. There are only two kinds of murder, first-degree and second-degree. Elizabeth Broderick committed first-degree murder, because under the law this is willful, intentional first-degree murder."

Kerry Wells continued flawlessly summarizing the events that occurred over the three-year period between 1986 and 1989, then she concluded, "She had the gun, she had the keys, she had the kids, the time was right. The fact is Dan and Linda weren't doing anything but sleeping in their own bed, and with killing in her heart and hatred in her heart, Elizabeth Broderick shot them. . . . Ladies and gentlemen," Wells added as her voice broke with emotion. "if that isn't murder, I don't know what is."

• 22 •

"He killed her before she killed him," Vivian Smith told the other jurors in the room. "He tormented her like an animal in a cage." She was surprised to see that almost no one agreed. She was, Vivian decided, the token older woman.

The young people were too young to understand how it would feel to be treated that way. One girl turned twenty-one during the trial. There was another girl and a guy who sided with her, but under pressure they were folding quickly and moving away. Everyone else wanted first-degree.

After a while they got hostile, and Vivian got angry. "Why don't we just ring for the bailiff?" she said. "You guys can say you want me kicked off the panel because I don't agree."

"No, you know we can't do that," the jury foreman told her.

For seven weeks Vivian had liked these people. They'd eaten lunch together, they'd become friends, they'd gone shopping together but they had never talked about Betty Broderick. Never even squeaked a word. They'd been told by the judge not to. Besides it was so mind-boggling that they'd wanted to get away from it.

Before the trial started, Vivian said to herself, *She's guilty as hell.* But when she saw how Betty had been taunted, how Dan wouldn't let up on her, she decided that this had done something to Betty.

At the end of the first day of deliberation Vivian held out for manslaughter. George, the jury foreman said, "I feel it should be first-degree for Linda, and second-degree for Dan." Then he threw his pencil down. "Dammit," he said. "I really feel it should be first-degree for both of them, but I'm willing to settle."

The girl at the other end of the table said, "I'll go to second-degree on Dan, but not on Linda." It went on like that. Finally they came around to Vivian again. "I'm still for manslaughter," Vivian said.

That night she couldn't sleep. She came downstairs and watched a tape of the interview that Betty had done on *20/20* when she was still being held in solitary confinement.

Vivian knew she wasn't supposed to watch it, but she needed help. She just kept going back to manslaughter in her heart. She needed to talk to someone about what she felt, and she couldn't talk to anyone. She couldn't talk to the eleven people on the jury, who were screaming and hollering at her, and she couldn't talk to her friends or family because she wasn't allowed to. So she came down at three in the morning and she thought, *Hell, I need to watch it now. I need to see if there's anything in this tape that could clear it up for me, that would make me feel everyone in the jury was right and I was wrong.*

It didn't work that way. Instead she tossed and turned the rest of the night, and found herself unable to deal with the other jurors' decision.

Vivian herself had two sons and one daughter. They were all grown up now. She'd worked on a switchboard as a long-distance operator before retiring. She'd had a wonderful marriage. It had felt to her like a thirty-year honeymoon. He had been her best friend, and if she never met anyone else after he died of a heart attack at fifty-five, that was okay with her. She'd had enough love for a lifetime.

Vivian Smith was one of those warm, upbeat women who believed you made your own happiness. God had been good to her, but as she saw it, he had not been good to Betty.

She thought about holding out for another trial. *But,* she thought, *if they do it again, maybe she'll get first-degree.* If she believed it would be a mistrial and Betty could go home to her boys, she'd have held out. But she kept worrying, *What if I only make it worse, what if I only make it worse?*

All the rest of that night she agonized. "Dammit," she said. "Betty was so honest that she hurt herself. She could have set it up to look like self-defense or she could have cried and said she was sorry to the jury. She could have pleaded temporary insanity. That would have saved her."

"Okay," Vivian said to her colleagues the next day. "Let's try to reenact it. Here's what I think happened. I want to get this thing settled. I think it was all done from one side of the room. I think she ripped the phone out because she was genuinely afraid Dan would call the police. I think she did develop the blanks in memory that she claims."

"Hey," one juror said. "I'd lie, too, if my life was on the line. I think she's lying." The other jurors kept hammering away at the idea of malice. "Anytime you walk into anyone's house with a gun, that's malice," the foreman insisted. "Do you agree that she had a gun?"

"Yes," Vivian said. "She had a gun!"

"Then that is malice," he shouted. "And if it's malice, it's not manslaughter."

"But she went up there to kill herself with the gun," Vivian insisted, "so it's not malice."

"She had the gun in her hand," the foreman shouted.

"Okay," Vivian said. "I have to agree she went into the room with the gun. Why don't we get the transcripts and hear her testimony again?"

The stenographer came in with the transcripts and read them out loud. They contained the obscene phone calls that Betty made on the children's answering machine. Everyone except Vivian started going back toward first-degree. "How can she love her children if she did that to them?" they said. "This is not an obscenity trial," Vivian answered. They took a break. Outside in the hall Vivian saw Kim standing with Helen Picard and crying.

"Why didn't Dan have an alarm system?" she asked when she went back into the room. "He seemed to be playing a daredevil game. He knew she had the gun, it was registered to her. Why didn't he get a court order to take it away? Why was he focusing on his own murder thirteen years earlier way back in the marriage encounter weekend? I think something was wrong with him. I think he wanted to drive her crazy, but he couldn't succeed. He wanted her to do things that made her look crazy, like driving into his front door. He played with the fire a little too much. Maybe he thought all she would ever do was call him names or maybe he really wanted to self-destruct.

"If it were up to me," Vivian finally said, "I would say to Betty, 'You're out on parole, but you have to report every single week and God be with you.' "

"If she had the gun, then it's malice," the rest of them kept saying.

"Then why have a trial?" Vivian asked. "Why have a defense? We know she had the gun, and if the gun automatically means its first-degree, why go through any of this?"

That night Vivian went home and cried again. She cried over everything. There was no one in there she could turn to for emotional support. She felt all alone and defeated. On the third day it still was a hung jury. *If there is another trial, she might do even worse,* Vivian thought again.

"We have to come to a verdict," the foreman said.

Finally Vivian agreed to compromise. "If you change from first- to second-degree in the deaths of both Dan and Linda, I'll change from manslaughter and go along with you." It wasn't that she felt it was second-degree. But she believed it was the best she could do for Betty.

"Tell her that my prayers are with her," Vivian told the bailiff as he led her out over the roof so that the press wouldn't see her crying. "I only hope the judge has enough compassion in his heart to give her the lightest sentence."

No one told Vivian Smith that if she had held out for manslaughter, the judge would have declared a second hung jury and Betty Broderick would probably have been set free.

On February 7, 1992, Judge Thomas Whelan thanked both sides for the excellent heated jobs they had both done. "This case has been a tragedy for everyone," he said, "most of all for the four Broderick children, who are orphans." Whelan paused and looked directly at Betty. "Everyone believes this case deserves punishment," he said. "As for the strong emotions, let us put them aside. They have gone on long enough, for over two years in my courtroom. This is a time for healing."

Then Whelan imposed the maximum possible sentence under the law for second-degree murder, thirty-two years to life in prison.

"These were separate acts of violence," he said, explaining his order for consecutive back-to-back fifteen-year sentences for each death. Before declaring that the court was in recess Whelan added two additional years for using a gun. "The physical evidence, which is uncontradicted, shows that she intentionally and deliberately aimed at both people."

Betty's father put his arm around Lee as two court deputies helped Betty up. "It's too long. It's too long," Lee sobbed. "She'll never get out. She'll die there."

Pale, expressionless, and swaying on her feet, Betty Broderick was led from the courtroom.

PART VII
• • •
Life Today

"We really were the perfect couple with the perfect dream, and even now, even in prison when I remember the old Dan, the one who told me he loved me and asked me to marry him every single day, it all comes back and I miss him so much."

—*Betty Broderick from prison, November 12, 1992*

• 1 •

Betty Broderick on Prison Life

"People ask me what it's like in prison, and I say it's just like the real world. You have people out there who are above you. You can be very comfortable. They can send you clothes, they can send you food, they can send you money, you can be extremely comfortable in here. But if you have no money, it's a very hard hustle and struggle, just like it is for homeless street people who have to steal shoes and steal jeans and steal coffee because they have nothing.

"You shop once a month in the little prison canteen. You can spend a hundred and fifty dollars from your credit account if you have it, and of course the more you buy, the more comfortable you are and the more you have to trade with other people.

"I had to buy my first pair of shoes from someone for forty dollars. I don't have any cash. No one does. So I buy forty dollars of canteen, cigarettes, coffee, whatever the lady wants, that's how I pay the lady the forty dollars for these sneakers.

"Breakfast is at six-thirty. Lunch is a box lunch all week long at eleven. Some kind of bologna or something. Dinner's at four or five. It varies, because you have to go by unit. Lights out by eleven o'clock, I think. Nobody ever stays up that late anyway, because they all work and get up at five thirty.

"Before work you have to make your bed and clean your room every morning, because there's inspection like in the military, and the towels have to be folded just so, the blankets have to be folded just so. They come in and inspect.

"I am working the night shift, which starts at two-thirty in the afternoon, so I stay behind and clean the room. I'm the housewife.

I clean for everybody, and that's like unheard of in here, but I don't mind.

"What I like is the peace and quiet when they're all gone. In the other rooms one person does the floor, one person does the toilets, one person does the shower, one person does the sinks, one person does the windows, one does the locker room.

"I said, 'You know what? You all leave and I'll do it.' I work from two-thirty in the afternoon till ten o'clock at night. They come home at two-thirty. All you have to do is pass inspection in the morning at nine o'clock. When inspection is over, you can leave your stuff out, you can mess up your bed and be a little messy. But you've got to get that room totally pulled together for inspection, and five is the highest score. We get five every time.

"It gives me some quiet time, so I play housewife, just like I always did. Six people in this little room. You could get killed, run over, 'cause they're all running out of bed to the toilet and to the shower. Six people in this one tiny little room. They're all in a hurry. There's one toilet, and one shower, in little stalls next to each other. And then two sinks and two mirrors. But one of my roommates takes two hours to put on her makeup. In women's prison, can you believe it, there is hairspray and eye shadow and eyeliner, because they all have all kinds of affairs going. I'm like, 'Please, I wouldn't spend that time on makeup in the real world.'

"But they have these affairs with each other. Some of them have wives and they get married and things. Lesbianism flourishes here. It's wonderful, I just crack up. It's against the rules, but they can't stop it. When people are discovered, they get written up. I haven't been here long enough to really figure it out. I sit back and observe.

"The lesbian relationships I've seen so far are extremely abusive. You know, the one who plays the man calls the other one bitch, just like in the real world. I said to one of them, 'Does that mean that's how you think that men act, always in a bad mood and pissed off, and the wife does the laundry and is responsible for making the food for lunch and stuff?'

"They're all into lingerie in here. I wasn't even into lingerie in the real world. I didn't have time. They have Victoria's Secret, expensive lingerie, I couldn't believe it. And it's constant trauma, constant trauma, who's mad at who and who's calling who bitch, and who's cheating. And I'm like, 'Please, who could be bothered?'

"You always see a butch and a fem. The women don't just love each other. They have roles, definite roles. There's always the constant threat of 'Don't you look at anyone.' Two friends of mine are wives. One wife got a new roommate the other night. So the other husband marched her tough ass down there—you should have seen the walk on her—and she said, 'I just want you to know that you're in the room with my wife.' And the other one said, 'Okay, okay. You don't have to worry about me. I won't touch her. I won't look at her.' She was like, 'I just want to get that straight.' So she came strutting back. I was sitting next to her, and she said, 'I told her the way it is.'

"I worked with two of these people. And if the girl of the group was talking to anyone else, the husband would be like, 'Don't think I didn't see that.' It's incredible. Getting in a bad mood and all pissed off over nothing. I'm like, 'What is this? You're not allowed to talk to anybody?'

"I've been in four different rooms already. I've had all kinds of roommates. I've had a wife that lives above me. I've had a husband that lives across from me. But they're not wife and husband to each other. They're all lesbians in my room except the Spanish one. She's a drug dealer. Maybe she's a lesbian drug dealer, for all I know. But all I know so far is she's a drug dealer.

"We have these little heaters to make coffee and heat up noodles and spaghetti and stuff. This is the most awful story. One woman is in the infirmary right now. All over some other woman, homosexual stuff. She was unfaithful. The other woman heated up sugar, made a paste with Kool-Aid and sugar and boiling water. A paste on purpose, so it would stick. She threw it in the girl's face, then beat the shit out of her, knocked all her teeth out. I think she's disfigured for life. I haven't seen her yet. She's been in the hospital with severe burns and all that. And she was the prettiest girl. Hot little body and blond hair. She was sweet. Isn't that a shame, fucked around.

"As I said, money and possessions are the other big issues.

"You have to lock everything up. You can't go to bed at night and

229

sleep with your shoes next to your bed. Someone will steal those shoes, and obviously they will get caught with them, right? So they sell them. They pay a debt with them, and that person pays her debt with them. It only takes them half an hour and these shoes have gone through five people, so they can't prosecute the person who ends up with these shoes because she got them honestly.

"They're always trying to sell watches. I would never try to buy these things because you know they've been stolen from someone else. No, thank you. And if I got my stuff in here, any of it, just like I described, it would disappear. I'd find it or they'd find it on someone. The cops don't even get involved with trying to get anything back. They just leave it all to the inmates. They beat each other up and steal things. It's very much fend-for-yourself. So the less that I have in here, the better off I am, and I'm glad I don't smoke or do drugs, because that's where people get into big problems always.

"One good thing is they have these family visits, immediate family. My children can come here and stay five days in a little house with me. They have beds and TVs and kitchens. The family brings all the food and you cook. Right now I'm trying to get Rhett here, and it's so difficult, because this prison is so far from San Diego. If it was close, I'd have the help and support of Brad.

"Someone needs to deliver him and the groceries and come back for him four or five days later and put him back on the plane. Up here I don't have that support. I don't want him going all by himself, and I don't want my other children making this drive up here. It's ten hours from San Diego in the heat. I don't want my kids out there on those roads. I've done this drive going through the Sierras in the summer, it's a killer. It's extremely hot. Cars overheat, they run out of gas. It's a major, treacherous drive. It takes a whole day in each direction.

"Rhett said, 'I can do it by myself, Mom.' I'm like, you know, this spunky little kid probably could. I don't want him doing it, but he could do it. He says, 'I'll change planes. I'll get a cab and I'll stop and buy the groceries.' He would, he's that spunky, he really would. That kid would do anything. He believes he can do anything and he can do anything. He's a wonderful kid, and no one is ever going to tell him different about his mother and father ever.

"He knows what went on, and he knows it as sure as the nose on his face, and no one is ever going to tell him that it went any other way, because he knows how it really went.

"He says, 'Well, you know, Mom, Kathy Broderick always says you're unstable.' I say, unstable, huh. You want to see me unstable, fuck with my kids. I can get so unstable so fast. I said, 'Yes, fuck with my kids, I get real unstable.'

"I told people subsequent to this whole thing, the number-one law of nature when you go into the woods or when you go into the jungle or anything—and life is a jungle out there—is don't get between a mother and her babies, even by mistake, because you're going to get hurt. Even the nicest, calmest, most normally tame animal or person will get crazy if you threaten its babies.

"It's not a thought process, it's a switch. Dogs, bears, snakes, and people. When I was a little kid, we had robins' nests on the porch of our house. Robins are not aggressive birds at all. But let a bunch of kids go near a robin's nest, and the mother robin will come down and try to poke their eyes out.

"If I had had my kids, oh, God, none of this would ever have happened. The longer I'm in here, the more I start building a life here, until something reminds me, until something calls me back, and then it's always the terrible, aching longing in the pit of my stomach for my kids and my husband the way he used to be.

"It was such a waste of everyone's life, especially my kids'. Because I'm older, I really had my life, a full, lovely life, a nice childhood, a good education, I married the man of my dreams and raised these four lovely children, but my poor kids, they missed out. They got robbed. I never once cried over the verdict. I only cry for my children."

EPILOGUE

I have entered Betty's world, and I have left it, both sadder and with a renewed sense of my own good fortune, for in the ambiguity and contradictions that are Betty Broderick, like so many other women, I have found a mirror for some part of my own soul.

Again and again as I traveled down that dark path, I found myself startled by the paradoxes. Betty was a woman who killed the man she loved to keep the dream of him alive. A woman who finally found her lost freedom behind bars, the ultimate hostess with the sailor's tongue. She was at once a devoted mother and a trapped housewife. She was also a dependent girl inside a middle-aged woman, with a rage so primitive that it ended in murder.

Betty Broderick was able to give up an oceanfront home in La Jolla for a tiny gray prison cell without missing a beat, but she couldn't give up the memory of the Dan Broderick she once loved.

I have heard people say that Betty gave herself to Dan. They are right. She literally gave herself away. There was no separate self, because the boundaries had merged. In her mind she was Dan Broderick and he was her. He had become the monster inside her. By killing him she reclaimed herself.

If I believed in exorcism, I'd listen to Betty's voice and the language on those tapes and I'd point to the fact that she killed Dan thirteen years to the day after he expressed the fear that he would be killed.

If I believed that Greek tragedies foretold the modern future, I'd point to Jason and Medea and say that nothing is ever really new. Only the generations change.

If I believed that this book had a simple moral lesson for women of our time, I'd say, never give yourself away. Never love so much that the loss of it can separate you from yourself.

But this is not an Anne Rice novel, a Greek tragedy, or a contemporary morality play. In real life, wisdom is easier in retrospect.

In many ways they did appear to be the perfect couple, with the same goals and values. They were also the fatal couple, doomed to destroy the dream they had created.

This is more than a deadly divorce, more than an American dream that self-destructed. This is a revisiting of age-old emotions. Love, jealousy, greed, passion, maternal instinct, animal rage, and the wish to be saved.

They are forces that always exist. Now and then they collide. Sometimes they gather force and explode, exposing the lonely beast in each of us that prowls beneath the thin veneer of civilization.

For Dan and Betty Broderick, when events and emotions swirled out of control with hurricane force, what was left of their family was irretrievably scattered like ashes in the wind.

Today Betty and each of her children remain apart. The once picture-perfect American dream has been lost forever. Kim maintains a small apartment in San Diego. She is still going to school.

Lee, who was never put back in her father's will, works in a restaurant and is struggling to support herself at minimum wage.

Danny is back in La Jolla with Helen Picard, and Rhett is living in the Midwest with one of Betty's brothers and his family.

Betty continues to adjust to a world that most of us would find unimaginable.

Her first prison job was handing out uniforms. After that for a while she worked on what she called the chain gang, digging ditches all day in 105- to 120-degree heat. Today she works as a porter, straightening the chairs, emptying the ashtrays, mopping the floors, and sweeping them clean of ashes.

This is the Cinderella story in reverse. The fairy tale with the unhappy ending. Yet in another sense Betty Broderick has come full circle and returned home to the cheerfulness and the good-natured acceptance that characterized her early personality.

"It's the best job here," she says. "I love it. Because I work from two-thirty to ten-thirty, I have time in the morning to do the laundry and watch morning TV. I'm a housewife again. I'd walk the dog if I had one."

Betty works forty hours a week and earns eleven dollars a month. I knew that money was important even in prison, just for basic comforts. When I realized how difficult it was for her to earn it, I thought she might ask me to pay her for the interviews. I would have told her that I couldn't, because it was in conflict with my journalistic ethics. But she never asked. In fact she did exactly the opposite. "My roommates all thought I was getting paid for this book," she said. "I told them, 'No, if I need money I'll get it the right way, the way I always have: I'll earn it.' "

Nor did she ever ask me if she could review the manuscript. She trusted me.

My husband, on the other hand, did read the manuscript before it went to press.

"Well," I asked when he had finished, "do you still think she was crazy?"

"No," he answered. "I think she was intentionally and sadistically driven out of control, not just by Dan Broderick but with the complicity of the divorce courts. Actually I like her."

One of the most recent letters Betty sent me contained a letter from Kim. It was written on the airplane returning from her appearance on the *Oprah Winfrey* show. In it Kim said she had never had the chance to say a lot of things that she really wanted to say. "I guess it's good for ratings to pit me against you," Kim wrote, "but I'm really not against you."

There were, Kim added, many things she still disagreed with Betty about, but she said, "I do agree that you were a fantastic mother . . . extremely fun, beautiful, intelligent and that you gave us two hundred percent of yourself."

Kim also said that the *Oprah* show made it look as if she hadn't visited Betty because she didn't want to. She assured Betty that wasn't the case at all. The trip had just been hard to arrange.

The bottom line, Kim wrote, is "we miss you, we love you, and I personally don't want to be mad at you anymore." She said she was reassured by seeing the tape of *Oprah*'s prison interview with her mother and would try to visit often because she now understood that not seeing her must be painful for Betty. Kim ended the letter by printing the words *I love you, Mom* in large capital letters . . .

Even Kim, the most publicly damning and least forgiving of Betty's children, clearly cares deeply for her. She is still torn between conflicting loyalties. She is still struggling to come to terms with the double loss and still trying to understand her mother. For me, understanding Betty Broderick continues to be an ongoing process.

It was not until months after I left her at the prison and ran barefoot along the beach for both of us that her old friend, Anne Dick, published a letter in a San Diego newspaper saying that Betty had nothing and asking friends to contribute whatever they could to her canteen fund so that she could buy toothpaste, shampoo, coffee, soap, and other personal items. She had never told me.

The next time Betty called me collect from prison, I asked her if it was true that she had no money for these items. She said her mother had sent one check for ten dollars and that sometimes Brad sent money, but she hated to ask him.

It was September fifth, the day that Danny started high school back in La Jolla. I knew how much she wanted to be there. I had just come back from taking my own little son to his first day of kindergarten.

Suddenly I felt so rich in my good fortune that it hurt. When we got off the phone, I sat down and wrote a check to the prison canteen for five hundred dollars. It wasn't much, but it was a gesture of friendship from one woman, or perhaps from one mother to another. I wanted her to have what the other prisoners had.

Several days later I received a letter. She thanked me again and again. Then she told me she had gotten special permission to divide the check in half and send two hundred fifty dollars to each of her boys.

"The girls don't need it," she wrote, "because they have my jewelry and stuff. But in all the time since 1989 I haven't been able to give anything to my boys."

My first reaction was, *Oh, no, I wanted you to have that for yourself for soap and shampoo and toothpaste and shoes.* It took a moment before I realized that there was something she needed more than what I considered the basic necessities. It was the ability to give to her children and in that moment, however brief, to feel like a mother again.

Suddenly I recalled the last thing Betty said to me before I left the prison: "My job, my life, my duty on earth was to raise, educate, and care for my children."

It was the only time during our three days together that I had ever seen her cry.

ABOUT THE AUTHOR

LORETTA SCHWARTZ-NOBEL numbers among her awards the Columbia School of Journalism Award, the Robert F. Kennedy Award, the Women in Communication Award, the American Bar Association Award, the Penny Missouri Award, and the National Society of Professional Journalists Award. A resident of Pennsylvania, she has authored the Edgar-nominated true-crime work *Engaged to Murder, A Mother's Story* (with Mary Beth Whitehead), *Starving in the Shadow of Plenty,* and *The Baby Swap Conspiracy.*